Reading
Connections 3
From Academic Success to Everyday Fluency

Andrew E. Bennett

HEINLE
CENGAGE Learning™

Australia • Brazil • Japan • Korea • Mexico • Singapore • Spain • United Kingdom • United States

HEINLE
CENGAGE Learning™

Reading Connections 3:
From Academic Success to Everyday Fluency
Andrew E. Bennett

Publisher, the Americas, Global, and Dictionaries:
Sherrise Roehr
Acquisitions Editor: Tom Jefferies
Senior Development Editor: Yeny Kim
Director of US Marketing: Jim McDonough
Senior Product Marketing Manager: Katie Kelley
Academic Marketing Manager: Caitlin Driscoll
Director of Global Marketing: Ian Martin
Director of Content and Media Production:
Michael Burggren
Senior Content Product Manager:
Maryellen E. Killeen
Senior Print Buyer: Mary Beth Hennebury

Images: All images: (c) istockphoto.com

For product information and technology assistance, contact us at
Cengage Learning Customer & Sales Support, 1-800-354-9706

For permission to use material from this text or product, submit all requests online at **www.cengage.com/permissions**
Further permissions questions can be emailed to
permissionrequest@cengage.com

ISBN-13: 978-1-111-34864-9
ISBN-10: 1-111-34864-2

Heinle
20 Channel Center Street
Boston, MA 02210
USA

Cengage Learning is a leading provider of customized learning solutions with office locations around the globe, including Singapore, the United Kingdom, Australia, Mexico, Brazil and Japan. Locate your local office at
international.cengage.com/region

Cengage Learning products are represented in Canada by Nelson Education, Ltd.

Visit Heinle online at **elt.heinle.com**
Visit our corporate website at **www.cengage.com**

Printed in China
2 3 4 5 6 7 14 13 12 11 10

Contents

Contents

Introduction

Reading Connections 3 Overview

Reading Connections 3 combines integrated skill building and interesting content. The book contains 20 units based on a variety of modern topics. At the core of each unit is a reading passage, with interconnected vocabulary, listening, speaking, and writing activities. This comprehensive method allows students' English to rapidly improve. At the same time, engaging topics keep students interested and motivated while they learn.

Following are the features found in each unit of *Reading Connections 3*.

Pre-Reading Questions

This exercise includes three simple questions about the topic. It's designed to get students to start thinking about the topic for a few minutes. The exercise can be done in pairs, or the entire class can discuss the questions together.

Consider the Topic

This pre-reading exercise gives each student a chance to register his or her opinion about three statements related to the topic. The exercise helps make students more active and interested learners.

Reading Passage

The core component of each unit is an article about a modern topic. The topics are from a wide range of fields, including technology, health, science, modern lifestyles, sports, the environment, and more. This variety reflects the wide range of our daily literacy experiences and the breadth of issues facing us in the 21st century.

Each article in *Reading Connections 3* is about 400 words long. The vocabulary and grammar are carefully controlled, to improve comprehension and allow for focused instruction. The unit's target vocabulary words and phrases (which are tested in the Vocabulary Building and Phrase Building exercises) are bolded for easy reference.

Above the article is an audio CD icon. Next to it is a track number, indicating the track on the audo CD where students can listen to a recording of the article. Beneath the article is a glossary with definitions of the article's challenging words and phrases. The definitions are written in simplified English.

Questions about the Reading

There are five multiple choice comprehension questions. A wide variety of question types are used, including main idea, detail, vocabulary in context, and more.

Writing about the Article

This exercise gives students a chance to write short responses to questions about the article. To make things easier, the first few words of each answer are given. Each answer should be one sentence long.

Vocabulary Building

In this exercise, the unit's eight target vocabulary words are tested. The target words were selected for their usefulness and frequency of use. They are the words students are going to use and encounter over and over when speaking, reading, and writing English.

Phrase Building

This exercise tests the unit's three target phrases. It is in a "cloze passage" format. Phrases should be used only once, and students should make sure to use the correct word form. Note that there are four phrases but only three blanks. The extra phrase is there to reduce the impact of guessing.

Listening Exercise

The three questions in this exercise are based on a short conversation (about 80 words long) between two people. The conversation, which is recorded on the audio CD, is related to the unit's topic. (The track number is written next to the audio CD icon.) Not only is this exercise good practice for strengthening general listening skills, but it's also excellent practice for tests such as TOEIC and TOEFL.

Listening Activity

This activity is based on a short talk (about 80 words long). Each talk, which is related to the unit's topic, is recorded on the audio CD. (The track number is written next to the audio CD icon.) A variety of talk types are used, including information announcements, advertisements, introductions, and others. This activity gives students practice listening for key details, just as they would in the real world.

Discussion Questions

Now it's time for students to discuss questions related to the unit's topic. As they've already read an article and listened to a conversation and short talk about the topic (in addition to doing many other exercises), it's time for students to share their own ideas. The three questions in this exercise can be discussed in pairs, or the class can discuss the questions together.

Discussion Activity

This is the final exercise in each unit. Groups of classmates work together on a discussion activity. Simple directions for the activity are given, and a model example is provided to help students start talking.

Reading Connections **Program Overview**

Reading Connections is a NEW five-level series designed to develop the language and fluency necessary for success in real world and academic settings. The following pages highlight and explain key features of the *Reading Connections* program.

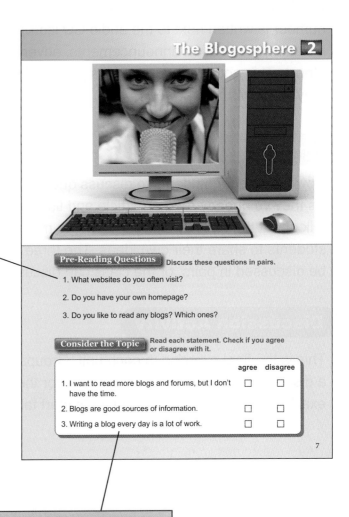

Pre-Reading questions designed for pair, group, or class discussion introduce the unit topic for increased comprehension of the reading to follow.

Consider the Topic sections give students the opportunity to create valuable connections between the reading topic and their own lives.

Unique and engaging readings, including contemporary topics such as **space colonies** and **"going carbon neutral,"** connect academic content to real world fluency.

Reading Passage 🔊 Disc 1, Track 4

1 Blogs (short for "weblogs") have grown into one of the Net's most important types of websites. There are now more than 100 million blogs, published by office workers, singers, businesses, and everyone in between. Blog posts often include links to other blogs, forming strong online communities. Altogether,
5 the Internet's **massive** collection of blogs is known as the "blogosphere."

Besides being free, blogs are easy to **maintain** – two big reasons for their popularity. Beneath the main banner are entries posted by the blog writer, or blogger. New entries **appear** at the top, so posts are listed in the order that they were written. Besides text, bloggers can add photos, sounds, videos,
10 and web links. Plus, blogs usually allow readers to add comments. When the blogger or other readers respond, it can lead to interesting conversations.

A blog may be about someone's daily life, job, hobbies, or any other topic. Someone interested in LCD TVs might start a blog about them, posting articles, reviews,
15 and his or her opinions. So, blogs are **resources** which are **informative**, yet personal. In the Internet age, that's a key **combination** which attracts readers.

The power of blogs to reach a wide audience is well known. Many celebrities use blogs to post news,
20 making traditional press releases less popular. Reporters track comments on the blogosphere to **measure** the public's reaction to events. And, politicians use blogs to voice their ideas.

In the USA, more than 50% of Internet users enjoy reading blogs. That has
25 **caught the eye of** a lot of businesses. Some companies hire bloggers to write about products. Bloggers can also make money by hosting ads from firms like Amazon. And, through programs like Google's AdSense, ads are placed on a blog based on its keywords. Bloggers can also set up deals with companies. So, for example, a blog about cats may display a pet food company's banner.

---
[7] banner – sign (usually with a group or company's name on it)
[18] audience – group of people who see something
[23] politician – someone in the government (Ex: a president)

8

30 With so many money-making **opportunities**, popular bloggers can earn $1,000 per month or more. Some even make a full-time living from their blogs. The key is to add new content **on a regular basis**. You want people to know that your site is useful and **up to date**. That may mean spending several hours a day creating new content. If a blog's traffic reaches 2,000
35 daily visitors, it's a sign that you're a big hit in the blogosphere.

---
[34] traffic – visitor level

Questions about the Reading Choose the best answer.

1. ( ) What is the main idea?
   (A) It takes a lot of time to add content to a blog.
   (B) Celebrities keep in touch with fans through blogs.
   (C) Blogs have become a popular type of website.
   (D) Comments from blog readers lead to conversations.

2. ( ) What is a blogger?
   (A) A popular blog writing style
   (B) A special kind of blog entry
   (C) A person who runs a blog
   (D) A banner at the top of a blog

3. ( ) Why are press releases less popular than they used to be?
   (A) They are too much trouble to set up.
   (B) The media is paying less attention to the Net.
   (C) Politicians prefer to track events through blogs.
   (D) People are using blogs to release news.

4. ( ) Which of the following is true about blogs?
   (A) About one-third of US Web users like reading them.
   (B) A popular blog may attract 2,000 visitors per day.
   (C) There are more than 100 billion blogs on the Net.
   (D) More than 50% of all new blogs come from the USA.

5. ( ) What does the article say about making money from blogs?
   (A) Writing about products is the easiest way to get rich.
   (B) Most bloggers treat blogs as their full-time job.
   (C) Hosting ads from Amazon is one way to earn money.
   (D) It's almost impossible to earn $1,000 per month.

9

Questions about the Reading sections in every unit assess student comprehension of the passage while teaching valuable reading skills such as finding the main idea, looking for detail, learning vocabulary in context, and making inferences. Perfect for **critical thinking** practice!

Writing about the Article activities ask students to write short answers in complete sentences, assessing reading comprehension while practicing writing skills.

Phrase Building activities assess and apply the unit's target phrases in a cloze exercise.

Writing about the Article Answer each question based on the article.

1. Besides text, what can people add to a blog?

2. What do politicians use blogs for?

3. What is the key to a successful blog?

Vocabulary Building Choose the best word to fill in each blank.

1. This little box _____ the street's air quality.
   (A) places (B) releases (C) measures (D) reaches

2. Hybrid cars get their power from a _____ of gas and electricity.
   (A) celebrity (B) community (C) comment (D) combination

3. Our new ads will _____ in magazines starting next month.
   (A) appear (B) write (C) attract (D) hire

4. When I got home from vacation, I found a _____ pile of mail waiting for me.
   (A) popular (B) traditional (C) massive (D) full-time

5. My local library is a great _____. It carries 20 different newspapers.
   (A) content (B) resource (C) website (D) link

6. You should go to the office party. It's a good _____ to get to know your colleagues better.
   (A) conversation (B) reaction (C) message (D) opportunity

7. I found the article highly _____. It taught me a lot about fashion design.
   (A) informative (B) regular (C) free (D) main

8. I spend about 10 hours a week _____ my website.
   (A) responding (B) allowing (C) maintaining (D) including

10

Phrase Building Write the correct phrase in each blank. (Remember to use the correct word form.)

● catch the eye of ● on a regular basis ● act as ● up to date

Ayana runs a blog about gardening. She adds new posts _____ (at least three times a week), and she has several hundred readers. Ayana frequently visits the Net's biggest gardening sites. That helps her keep the blog _____ with the latest news. Sometimes, Ayana adds photos of her personal garden to her blog. One of those posts _____ a local business. They were so impressed with Ayana's work that they invited her to design their company's garden.

Listening Exercise Disc 1, Track 5

Listen to the conversation. Then, answer the following questions.

1. ( ) What did the woman add to her blog today?
   (A) Funny pictures of her dog
   (B) News about South America
   (C) Photos from a vacation
   (D) A link to the man's site

2. ( ) Why hasn't the man visited the woman's blog recently?
   (A) He was having computer problems.
   (B) He has been working on his own blog.
   (C) He can't find the link to her blog.
   (D) He wasn't feeling very well.

3. ( ) What does the man want to do?
   (A) Raise another dog or cat
   (B) Learn how to start a blog
   (C) Ask his friend about her trip
   (D) Use the woman's video

11

Vocabulary Building exercises test the unit's target vocabulary in exercises designed both to assess comprehension and apply high-frequency terms to meaningful contexts.

Listening Exercises in every unit offer thematically-related conversations in MP3 format on audio CD or online that assess student comprehension for test-preparation and for building fluency.

Listening Activity sections prompt students to listen and record key details from a short talk offered in a variety of formats such as advertisements and introductions to build real-world fluency.

Unit 2

Listening Activity Disc 1, Track 6

Listen to the report. Then, fill in the information in the chart.

1. What is becoming easier to do?	
2. How did most people go online in the 1990s?	
3. Name two other devices that can go online.	
4. Name one thing people can do while driving.	
5. What can bloggers upload using a phone?	

Discussion Questions

1. People write about many topics on blogs, including hobbies, medical topics, and so on. What's a topic you'd love to read about on a blog?

2. Some people read news blogs instead of newspapers. Is that a good idea? Why or why not?

3. As blogs and other news sites become more popular, people are reading fewer magazines, newspapers, and books. How about you? Do you still read a lot of printed materials?

Discussion Activity

Working with several classmates, plan a new blog. First, decide what the blog will be about. What will its name be? What will be special about it? (Will you post a lot of photos? Videos?) Finally, think of some ways to earn money from the site. After you're done, tell the rest of the class about your blog.

Example: Our blog will be about cell phones. Each person in our group has two phones, so we have a lot to write about....

12

Discussion Questions encourage students to discuss the unit's theme in pairs, groups, or as a class to form opinions on the topic based on their work with the reading passage and the communicative activities.

The *Discussion Activity* at the end of each unit gives students clear directions to work together towards one goal related to the unit's theme to solidify and apply target skills.

Audio recordings of all student book readings available in MP3 files on audio CD and FREE online at elt.heinle.com/readingconnections

Also **available**:

Assessment CD-ROM with Exam*View*® allows teachers to create tests and quizzes quickly easily!

Scope and Sequence

	Title	Theme	Reading Skills	Listening Exercise & Activity	Discussion Activity
1	Stem Cells	Health	Identifying details; using vocabulary in context	Conversation about stem cell therapies; announcement about a lecture	Debating the pros and cons of stem cell research
2	The Blogosphere	The Internet	Identifying the main idea and details; using vocabulary in context	Conversation about a blog; report about online trends	Planning a new blog
3	Organic Food	Nutrition	Identifying details; recognizing suggestions and implications	Conversation about organic food; advertisement for a supermarket	Debating eating for good health vs. eating for pleasure
4	Franchises	Careers	Identifying details; using vocabulary in context	Conversation about opening a franchise; report about an upcoming trade fair	Planning a new franchise
5	Character Culture	Identity	Identifying the main idea and details; recognizing suggestions	Conversation about opening a bank account; report about a person changing his name	Inventing a character for a company
6	Language Change	Communication	Identifying details; using vocabulary in context	Conversation about a foreign language movie; report about an award for new words	Discussing ways to improve one's English

	Title	Theme	Reading Skills	Listening Exercise & Activity	Discussion Activity
7	The Pursuit of Perfection	Sports	Identifying the main idea and details; recognizing implications	Conversation about a star athlete; report about a retired athlete's rumored return	Debating whether athletes deserve high salaries
8	Bicycling around Taiwan	Traveling	Identifying details; understanding recommendations	Conversation about an upcoming trip; advertisement for a vacation package	Planning a trip with a group of friends
9	The End of Privacy	Social Issues	Identifying the main idea and details; recognizing suggestions	Conversation about a website; report about a new crime fighting system	Debating the importance of safety vs. freedom
10	Going Carbon Neutral	The Environment	Identifying details; recognizing implications	Conversation about reducing one's carbon output; report about a unique wedding	Making a trip carbon neutral
11	Yellow Dust Storms	Nature	Identifying details; using vocabulary in context; recognizing implications	Conversation about the weather; report about dust storms	Planning a program to help the environment
12	It pays to be the CEO.	Business	Identifying details; using vocabulary in context; recognizing suggestions	Conversation about a CEO; report about a company's salary structure	Debating the high salaries of CEOs

	Title	Theme	Reading Skills	Listening Exercise & Activity	Discussion Activity
13	London	World Cities	Identifying details; using vocabulary in context	Conversation about an airline booking; advertisement for a museum	Introducing your city to the world
14	Web 2.0	The Internet	Identifying the main idea and details; using vocabulary in context	Conversation about the Internet; report about a new website	Listing positive and negative aspects of the Internet
15	Troubled Stars	Entertainment	Identifying details; using vocabulary in context; recognizing implications	Conversation about child stars; report about a new charity	Making up a news report about a celebrity
16	M-Shaped Society	Social Issues	Identifying the main idea and details	Conversation about a job search; report about rising prices	Debating the lifestyles of the young generation
17	Space Colonies	Space	Identifying the main idea and details; recognizing suggestions	Conversation about a space agency; report about traveling to the moon	Talking about a new space colony
18	Office Gossip	The Workplace	Identifying details; using vocabulary in context	Conversation about a colleague; announcement about a merger between two companies	Playing the "grapevine" game

	Title	Theme	Reading Skills	Listening Exercise & Activity	Discussion Activity
19	Lost Arts	The Arts	Identifying details; recognizing suggestions	Conversation about an art fair; report about a traditional craft	Making a plan to promote traditional arts
20	Taiwan's Hi-Tech Future	The Future	Identifying details; using vocabulary in context; recognizing suggestions	Conversation about future careers; report about a survey of university students	Discussing what the world will be like in 100 years

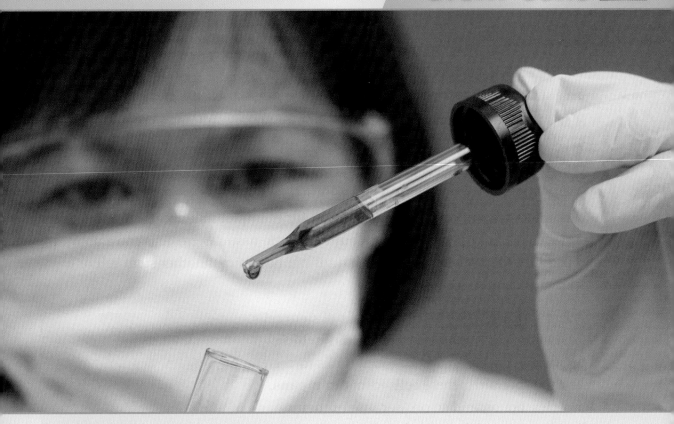

Discuss these questions in pairs.

1. What are some recent medical discoveries you've heard of or read about?

2. Which diseases are the most important to find cures for?

3. Do you know what stem cells are? What's special about them?

Consider the Topic Read each statement. Check if you agree or disagree with it.

	agree	disagree
1. More money should be put into medical research.	☐	☐
2. Cloning people is wrong, even if it's for medical purposes.	☐	☐
3. This century, we will cure most major diseases.	☐	☐

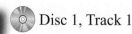

Reading Passage   Disc 1, Track 1

1   We are entering a golden age of medicine. Nearly every year, major
    breakthroughs are announced in the fight against disease. One of the most
    promising areas of research is in the use of stem cells. Although we have known
    about them for decades, the flood of breakthroughs in the field began in the late
5   1990s.

    A stem cell is a cell without a specific function. However, it has the ability to
    turn into any kind of specialized cell. So, for example, a stem cell could become
    a blood cell, neuron, or a cell that builds muscle tissue. Stem cells can also
    reproduce themselves through cell division, becoming another stem cell or a
10 specialized cell.

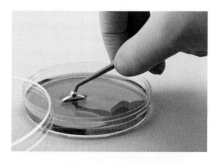

    Scientists largely focus on two kinds of stem cells.
    First, there are "embryonic stem cells," which
    divide and specialize after an embryo is formed.
    As they specialize, these cells form our **organs**,
15 muscles, bones, and so on. Because of their
    limitless **potential**, researchers feel embryonic
    stem cells hold the greatest hope for medical uses.

    As a person grows, he or she stores a number of stem cells in the tissues, blood,
    and other parts of the body. These "adult stem cells" assist the body **in the**
20 **event of** sickness or injury. **Depending on** where they are stored in the body,
    adult stem cells turn into a specific type of cell – for the blood, bones, and so on.
    Scientists are trying to figure out how to grow adult stem cells in a **laboratory**.
    If successful, they may be able to design therapies using a **patient's** own stem
    cells.

25 The potential medical uses of stem cells are incredible. Since the 1960s, doctors
    have performed bone marrow transplants, transferring stem cells from one
    person to another. This treatment has been used to battle leukemia and other
    diseases. The hope is that by using adult or embryonic stem cells, doctors will be
    able to treat many other serious illnesses. Parkinson's disease and Alzheimer's

---

³ promising - hopeful; having a good chance of succeeding
⁸ neuron – a type of cell found in the nervous system
¹³ embryo – an organism (still in the womb) in its very early stages of growth

30   disease may be among the first to be treated using stem cell therapies.

However, stem cell research is not without **controversy**. Many people are **opposed to** research on embryonic stem cells if it involves killing embryos to gather cells. There is also opposition to cloning humans or human body parts. However, scientists continue making amazing discoveries, even

35   when working under **restrictions**. They are successfully unlocking the secrets of stem cells, one by one.

33 cloning – making an exact copy

Questions about the Reading   Choose the best answer.

1. (   ) Which of the following is true about stem cells?
   (A) They are unable to reproduce themselves.
   (B) They do not have a specific function.
   (C) They can be easily grown in a laboratory.
   (D) They were only recently discovered.

2. (   ) Which of these is a current use of stem cells?
   (A) Treating Alzheimer's disease
   (B) Transplanting bone marrow
   (C) Curing Parkinson's disease
   (D) Growing new organs for a patient

3. (   ) What does the word *flood* in line 4 mean?
   (A) overflowing water
   (B) rising cost
   (C) serious damage
   (D) large numbers

4. (   ) The article does NOT say stem cells can turn into _____.
   (A) blood cells
   (B) neurons
   (C) embryonic cells
   (D) tissue cells

5. (   ) Which of the following is mentioned as a potential use of stem cells?
   (A) Curing serious diseases
   (B) Helping people change their appearance
   (C) Making people smarter and stronger
   (D) Finding a way to live forever

3

Writing about the Article
Answer each question based on the article.

1. What are the two kinds of stem cells researchers focus on?

   _____

2. Why are scientists trying to grow adult stem cells in laboratories?

   _____

3. Why are some people against embryonic stem cell research?

   _____

Vocabulary Building
Choose the best word to fill in each blank.

1. There is a lot of _____ about the effects of the hole in the ozone layer.
   (A) tissue   (B) controversy   (C) reproduction   (D) potential

2. There is a weight _____ for dogs living in the apartment building. They cannot be over 25 pounds.
   (A) breakthrough (B) organ   (C) restriction   (D) function

3. I'm supposed to meet my professor at the biology _____ at 3:00.
   (A) laboratory   (B) patient   (C) cell   (D) therapy

4. There have been many technological _____ in the past century that have improved our way of life.
   (A) diseases   (B) muscles   (C) controversies (D) breakthroughs

5. After visiting the emergency room, I was asked to fill out a _____ survey about the care I received.
   (A) stem   (B) reproduction (C) patient   (D) laboratory

6. She has a lot of _____ to succeed in school, but she is rather lazy.
   (A) potential   (B) division   (C) function   (D) restriction

7. The heart, liver, and lungs are all _____ in the human body.
   (A) bones   (B) organs   (C) patients   (D) injuries

8. Today, we learned how viruses _____ inside our bodies.
   (A) assist   (B) reproduce   (C) announce   (D) treat

Phrase Building Write the correct phrase in each blank.

● in the event of   ● one by one   ● depending on   ● opposed to

_____ how busy their parents are, older children may need to watch their younger siblings some of the time. While the older children may be _____ their role as babysitter at first, they usually learn to accept the responsibility. It also helps if the parents are willing to pay them for watching their younger brothers and sisters. Of course, it is very important that the child in charge knows who to contact _____ an emergency. This will help both the parents and their children feel at ease.

Listening Exercise   Disc 1, Track 2

Listen to the conversation. Then, answer the following questions.

1. (   ) Where did the man learn about stem cell therapies?
    (A) A website
    (B) A book
    (C) A newspaper
    (D) A medical journal

2. (   ) According to the woman, what will stem cell cures depend on?
    (A) The risk of making the illness worse
    (B) The types of cells affected by the disease
    (C) Doctors' interest in using them
    (D) Patients' willingness to be treated

3. (   ) How does the man feel about stem cell research?
    (A) Uncertain
    (B) Confused
    (C) Critical
    (D) Fascinated

Listening Activity   Disc 1, Track 3

Listen to the announcement. Then, fill in the information in the chart.

1. Who is hosting the lecture series?	
2. What is Dr. Bowman's occupation?	
3. What will be held after the lecture?	
4. Where will the lecture take place?	
5. Who does not have to pay to attend?	

Discussion Questions

1. Are you opposed to or in favor of gathering stem cells from embryos?

2. How do you feel about cloning people for their stem cells or body parts? Is it right or wrong?

3. Often, stem cell research which is funded by governments has many restrictions, while there are few restrictions on privately funded research. Do you think this is fair? Why or why not?

Discussion Activity

Hold a mini debate for and against stem cell research. First, divide into two groups: one for and one against. Next, prepare for the debate by writing down several points supporting your group's position. Finally, hold the mini debate.

Example: We support stem cell research. The main reason is it could help a lot of sick people....

Pre-Reading Questions

Discuss these questions in pairs.

1. What websites do you often visit?

2. Do you have your own homepage?

3. Do you like to read any blogs? Which ones?

Consider the Topic

Read each statement. Check if you agree or disagree with it.

	agree	disagree
1. I want to read more blogs and forums, but I don't have the time.	☐	☐
2. Blogs are good sources of information.	☐	☐
3. Writing a blog every day is a lot of work.	☐	☐

Reading Passage   Disc 1, Track 4

1 Blogs (short for "weblogs") have grown into one of the Net's most important types of websites. There are now more than 100 million blogs, published by office workers, singers, businesses, and everyone in between. Blog posts often include links to other blogs, forming strong online communities. Altogether,
5 the Internet's **massive** collection of blogs is known as the "blogosphere."

Besides being free, blogs are easy to **maintain** – two big reasons for their popularity. Beneath the main banner are entries posted by the blog writer, or blogger. New entries **appear** at the top, so posts are listed in the order that they were written. Besides text, bloggers can add photos, sounds, videos,
10 and web links. Plus, blogs usually allow readers to add comments. When the blogger or other readers respond, it can lead to interesting conversations.

A blog may be about someone's daily life, job, hobbies, or any other topic. Someone interested in LCD TVs might start a blog about them, posting articles, reviews,
15 and his or her opinions. So, blogs are **resources** which are **informative**, yet personal. In the Internet age, that's a key **combination** which attracts readers.

The power of blogs to reach a wide audience is well known. Many celebrities use blogs to post news,
20 making traditional press releases less popular. Reporters track comments on the blogosphere to **measure** the public's reaction to events. And, politicians use blogs to voice their ideas.

In the USA, more than 50% of Internet users enjoy reading blogs. That has
25 **caught the eye of** a lot of businesses. Some companies hire bloggers to write about products. Bloggers can also make money by hosting ads from firms like Amazon. And, through programs like Google's AdSense, ads are placed on a blog based on its keywords. Bloggers can also set up deals with companies. So, for example, a blog about cats may display a pet food company's banner.

---

[7] banner – sign (usually with a group or company's name on it)
[18] audience – group of people who see something
[23] politician – someone in the government (Ex: a president)

30   With so many money-making **opportunities**, popular bloggers can earn $1,000 per month or more. Some even make a full-time living from their blogs. The key is to add new content **on a regular basis**. You want people to know that your site is useful and **up to date**. That may mean spending several hours a day creating new content. If a blog's traffic reaches 2,000

35   daily visitors, it's a sign that you're a big hit in the blogosphere.

---

[34] traffic – visitor level

Questions about the Reading   Choose the best answer.

1. ( ) What is the main idea?
   (A) It takes a lot of time to add content to a blog.
   (B) Celebrities keep in touch with fans through blogs.
   (C) Blogs have become a popular type of website.
   (D) Comments from blog readers lead to conversations.

2. ( ) What is a blogger?
   (A) A popular blog writing style
   (B) A special kind of blog entry
   (C) A person who runs a blog
   (D) A banner at the top of a blog

3. ( ) Why are press releases less popular than they used to be?
   (A) They are too much trouble to set up.
   (B) The media is paying less attention to the Net.
   (C) Politicians prefer to track events through blogs.
   (D) People are using blogs to release news.

4. ( ) Which of the following is true about blogs?
   (A) About one-third of US Web users like reading them.
   (B) A popular blog may attract 2,000 visitors per day.
   (C) There are more than 100 billion blogs on the Net.
   (D) More than 50% of all new blogs come from the USA.

5. ( ) What does the article say about making money from blogs?
   (A) Writing about products is the easiest way to get rich.
   (B) Most bloggers treat blogs as their full-time job.
   (C) Hosting ads from Amazon is one way to earn money.
   (D) It's almost impossible to earn $1,000 per month.

Writing about the Article
Answer each question based on the article.

1. Besides text, what can people add to a blog?

   _____

2. What do politicians use blogs for?

   _____

3. What is the key to a successful blog?

   _____

Vocabulary Building
Choose the best word to fill in each blank.

1. This little box _____ the street's air quality.
   (A) places   (B) releases   (C) measures   (D) reaches

2. Hybrid cars get their power from a _____ of gas and electricity.
   (A) celebrity   (B) community   (C) comment   (D) combination

3. Our new ads will _____ in magazines starting next month.
   (A) appear   (B) write   (C) attract   (D) hire

4. When I got home from vacation, I found a _____ pile of mail waiting
   for me.
   (A) popular   (B) traditional   (C) massive   (D) full-time

5. My local library is a great _____. It carries 20 different newspapers.
   (A) content   (B) resource   (C) website   (D) link

6. You should go to the office party. It's a good _____ to get to know
   your colleagues better.
   (A) conversation (B) reaction   (C) message   (D) opportunity

7. I found the article highly _____. It taught me a lot about fashion
   design.
   (A) informative   (B) regular   (C) free   (D) main

8. I spend about 10 hours a week _____ my website.
   (A) responding   (B) allowing   (C) maintaining   (D) including

Phrase Building

Write the correct phrase in each blank. (Remember to use the correct word form.)

● catch the eye of ● on a regular basis ● act as ● up to date

Ayana runs a blog about gardening. She adds new posts _____ (at least three times a week), and she has several hundred readers. Ayana frequently visits the Net's biggest gardening sites. That helps her keep the blog _____ with the latest news. Sometimes, Ayana adds photos of her personal garden to her blog. One of those posts _____ a local business. They were so impressed with Ayana's work that they invited her to design their company's garden.

Listening Exercise

 Disc 1, Track 5

Listen to the conversation. Then, answer the following questions.

1. ( ) What did the woman add to her blog today?
   (A) Funny pictures of her dog
   (B) News about South America
   (C) Photos from a vacation
   (D) A link to the man's site

2. ( ) Why hasn't the man visited the woman's blog recently?
   (A) He was having computer problems.
   (B) He has been working on his own blog.
   (C) He can't find the link to her blog.
   (D) He wasn't feeling very well.

3. ( ) What does the man want to do?
   (A) Raise another dog or cat
   (B) Learn how to start a blog
   (C) Ask his friend about her trip
   (D) Use the woman's video

Listening Activity Disc 1, Track 6

Listen to the report. Then, fill in the information in the chart.

1. What is becoming easier to do?	
2. How did most people go online in the 1990s?	
3. Name two other devices that can go online.	
4. Name one thing people can do while driving.	
5. What can bloggers upload using a phone?	

Discussion Questions

1. People write about many topics on blogs, including hobbies, medical topics, and so on. What's a topic you'd love to read about on a blog?

2. Some people read news blogs instead of newspapers. Is that a good idea? Why or why not?

3. As blogs and other news sites become more popular, people are reading fewer magazines, newspapers, and books. How about you? Do you still read a lot of printed materials?

Discussion Activity

Working with several classmates, plan a new blog. First, decide what the blog will be about. What will its name be? What will be special about it? (Will you post a lot of photos? Videos?) Finally, think of some ways to earn money from the site. After you're done, tell the rest of the class about your blog.

Example: Our blog will be about cell phones. Each person in our group has two phones, so we have a lot to write about....

Pre-Reading Questions
Discuss these questions in pairs.

1. Do you try to live a healthy lifestyle? How so?

2. Have you ever tried organic food? What kinds?

3. What kinds of food are especially good for you?

Consider the Topic
Read each statement. Check if you agree or disagree with it.

	agree	disagree
1. I'm very careful about what I eat.	☐	☐
2. I don't mind paying more for food if it's healthier.	☐	☐
3. It's easy to find organic food where I live.	☐	☐

Reading Passage Disc 1, Track 7

1   Recently, food safety has become a very big issue. **Chemicals** top the list
     of things to look out for. Yet, in "conventional" farming, chemicals are
     frequently used to kill insects and fight plant diseases. Also, livestock such
     as pigs and chickens are fed antibiotics and growth hormones. Unfortunately,
5   many dangerous chemicals are then eaten by people who buy oranges, eggs,
     meat, and other foods. In response, more people are switching to organic
     food. It's good for our health and good for the environment.

     Organic farming is almost the **opposite** of conventional farming. Instead of
     chemicals, farmers use natural methods to deal with insects and diseases.
10   Livestock are not kept in small cages but are given space to walk around.
     Plus, they are fed neither antibiotics nor growth hormones. The soil is also
     better cared for. Only natural fertilizers are used, and crops are "rotated."
     That means a crop is only grown on a piece of land for a **season** or two. Then,
     a different crop is grown there for a short time. And so on.

15   Supporters of organic farming note its many
     benefits. **First and foremost**, it reduces the
     amount of chemicals that we're **exposed
     to**. Also, some studies suggest organic food
     is higher in **vitamins** and minerals than
20   conventional food. Supporters also **point out**
     that organic food **tastes** better. What's more,
     since the soil only receives natural fertilizers,
     it is kept healthy for future generations.

     Many kinds of organic food, including fruits, vegetables, and beans, are
25   showing up in supermarkets. We're also seeing hundreds of packaged foods
     using organic ingredients. For example, more and more stores are carrying
     organic cookies, cereal, and bread. However, their prices are often higher
     than those of conventional goods. That's because organic food takes more

---

² conventional – regular/traditional   ⁴ growth hormone – chemical that speeds up
³ livestock – farm animals   growth
⁴ antibiotic – something that kills bacteria   ¹² fertilizer – something added to soil to help
                                                    crops grow

29 **effort** to grow. However, prices are coming down, since demand is
growing and more farms are becoming organic.

As people in Asia, Europe, North America, and elsewhere see the
benefits of organic food, the global market continues to grow. In 2006, it
was worth $36.7 billion. That was an increase of 13.7% over the **previous**
year. The market is expected to be worth more than $67 billion within a
35 few years. As health and environmental stories make front page news,
that's good news for us all. Eating organically is a tasty way to make our
lives, and our planet, greener.

Questions about the Reading   Choose the best answer.

1. (   ) What does the article suggest about conventional farms?
   (A) They use hormones to kill insects.
   (B) They have few problems with plant diseases.
   (C) They are all switching to organic methods.
   (D) They use chemicals which may be dangerous.

2. (   ) What is true about livestock on organic farms?
   (A) Animals spend most of the day and night in cages.
   (B) They are fed very few growth hormones.
   (C) Livestock do not receive antibiotics.
   (D) Their lives are the same as on conventional farms.

3. (   ) According to some studies, what is organic food higher in?
   (A) Chemicals
   (B) Vitamins
   (C) Fertilizers
   (D) Hormones

4. (   ) Why are crops rotated?
   (A) To reduce farming costs
   (B) To increase the farm's size
   (C) To earn more money
   (D) To better care for the soil

5. (   ) What is stated about the prices of organic products?
   (A) They will continue to rise.
   (B) They are high because organic food is harder to grow.
   (C) They probably won't change.
   (D) They are the same as those of conventional products.

Writing about the Article
Answer each question based on the article.

1. What is the most important benefit of organic food?

   _____

2. What are some kinds of packaged organic food items?

   _____

3. How much was the organic market worth in 2006?

   _____

Vocabulary Building
Choose the best word to fill in each blank.

1. It's going to take a lot of _____ to move the sofa up the stairs.
   (A) effort   (B) safety   (C) growth   (D) soil

2. The _____ owner of the car had a dog. There's still some dog hair on the floor.
   (A) previous   (B) natural   (C) healthy   (D) dangerous

3. This fruit drink is healthy. It's high in _____ and has no added sugar.
   (A) chemicals   (B) vitamins   (C) methods   (D) studies

4. The paint is mixed with special _____ to make it waterproof.
   (A) diseases   (B) farmers   (C) chemicals   (D) generations

5. My boss said the report was the _____ of what he wanted. So, I had to completely redo it.
   (A) space   (B) benefit   (C) market   (D) opposite

6. Winter is the _____ when we get the most rain.
   (A) season   (B) planet   (C) amount   (D) environment

7. We travel to Tokyo _____. We have friends there and know some great restaurants in the city.
   (A) basically   (B) frequently   (C) differently   (D) organically

8. The ice cream _____ like coffee, but the box says it's chocolate.
   (A) tastes   (B) means   (C) cares   (D) deals

Phrase Building — Write the correct phrase in each blank.

● first and foremost   ● come down   ● exposed to   ● point out

Factory workers are _____ many kinds of chemicals every day. So, they have to pay special attention to safety. _____, a mask, work suit, and gloves must be worn at all times. If there's a tear in any of these pieces of gear, a worker must leave the floor immediately to have it replaced. Also, everyone needs to pay close attention to the equipment around them. They must _____ any problems they see (such as cracks or leaks) to a supervisor.

Listening Exercise   Disc 1, Track 8

Listen to the conversation. Then, answer the following questions.

1. (   ) Who thinks organic food tastes better?
   (A) The man
   (B) The man's colleague
   (C) The woman
   (D) The woman's friend

2. (   ) What is the man worried about?
   (A) The taste
   (B) The quality
   (C) The selection
   (D) The price

3. (   ) What does the woman suggest doing?
   (A) Only buying organic products
   (B) Trying one kind of organic vegetable
   (C) Asking Joe for advice about food
   (D) Going somewhere else to shop

Listening Activity Disc 1, Track 9

Listen to the advertisement. Then, fill in the information in the chart.

1. What kind of store is it?	
2. How many kinds of fruits and vegetables does it have?	
3. What kinds of desserts are sold there?	
4. How much is the discount?	
5. What will shoppers receive when spending $50?	

Discussion Questions

1. In recent years, we've seen many reports about food safety. Are you worried about the safety of the food you eat? Why or why not?

2. If organic food were cheaper, would you buy it more often? Explain your answer.

3. Although we know a lot about nutrition, many people still love to eat junk food. How about you?

Discussion Activity

In groups of four, hold a mini debate. On one side are two people in favor of very healthy diets. (That means no candy or soda, and only organic food.) On the other side are two people who feel we should eat whatever we want. (After all, we only live once!) First, each side should spend a few minutes deciding on reasons for its point of view. Then, hold the mini debate.

Example: We believe people should have healthy diets. You'll feel better and live longer....

Discuss these questions in pairs.

1. What are some famous international franchises? (Ex: Burger King)

2. What are some local franchises started by people in your country?

3. Besides restaurants, what other industries have franchises?

Consider the Topic

Read each statement. Check if you agree or disagree with it.

	agree	disagree
1. I prefer eating and shopping at franchises.	☐	☐
2. Prices at famous franchise restaurants are usually low.	☐	☐
3. Running a franchise is a good way to make money.	☐	☐

1 Well-known companies are powered by their
names and reputations. When people walk into a
Subway sandwich shop in Tokyo, Rome, or Miami,
they know exactly what they're getting. Through
5 franchising, an investor can **tap into** this brand
power by opening a Subway of his or her own. The
risk is low, and the **rewards** can be big. No wonder
franchising is such a successful business model.

Franchising has been around for more than 100 years,
10 but its popularity took off in the 1950s. Leading the
trend were fast food restaurants like McDonald's.
These days, there are **franchises** in more than 85 industries, including dry
cleaning, hotels, and real estate. It's very big business. In the USA, there are
some 760,000 franchises, totaling more than $1.5 trillion in yearly revenues.

15 There are two sides in a franchise: the franchisor (the owner of the business
system) and the franchisee (the person who **licenses** the system). After
signing a "franchise agreement," the franchisee pays a fee. He or she also
pays for equipment, supplies, and, if necessary, building costs. The total
investment usually ranges from $10,000 to $1,000,000. After the business
20 opens, the franchisee also pays a percentage of sales revenues (called a
royalty) to the franchisor. **Marketing** fees must also be paid.

In return, the franchisee receives many benefits. Training is among the
most common ones. It includes everything from dealing with customers
to understanding the company's standards. The franchisor also handles
25 advertising. On top of that, there's the benefit of the brand reputation that the
company has built up. All these benefits make the risk of opening a franchise
much smaller than that of starting a business **from scratch**.

However, a franchise can also have **drawbacks**. If a customer at a single
restaurant gets sick, it may hurt every franchise in the system. Running a

---

⁵ investor – person who spends money (on a business, stock, etc.) to make more money
¹⁰ take off – quickly grow

30 franchise also means closely following the company's standards. So, one has to **give up** a degree of **independence**. You have to do things their way and **trust** that the system will work.

If you want to earn a lot of money from the business, you have to work hard. Also, remember that the monthly royalty must be paid, even if you
35 are losing money. **Nevertheless**, there are thousands of opportunities in franchising. They will surely grow as brand recognition becomes more important in the global economy.

[35] opportunity – chance   [36] recognition – awareness

Questions about the Reading   Choose the best answer.

1. (   ) What type of franchise is NOT mentioned in the article?
   (A) Hotels
   (B) Restaurants
   (C) Dry cleaners
   (D) Clinics

2. (   ) Around how many franchises are there in the USA?
   (A) 85
   (B) 100
   (C) 760,000
   (D) 1,500,000,000,000

3. (   ) What must a franchisee pay to the franchisor after opening the business?
   (A) Royalty payments
   (B) Employee salaries
   (C) Equipment fees
   (D) Building costs

4. (   ) What is NOT a benefit enjoyed by a franchisee?
   (A) Advertising handled by the franchisor
   (B) Brand reputation of the franchise
   (C) A high level of independence
   (D) Training from the franchisor

5. (   ) What does the phrase *built up* in line 26 mean?
   (A) Bought
   (B) Hired
   (C) Grown
   (D) Believed

Writing about the Article
Answer each question based on the article.

1. When did franchising become very popular?

   _____

2. How much would the total investment be for a low-cost franchise?

   _____

3. What may happen to a restaurant franchise if a customer gets sick?

   _____

Vocabulary Building
Choose the best word to fill in each blank.

1. You can _____ Ms. Zhang. She is a very honest person.
   (A) trust   (B) remember   (C) train   (D) range

2. As a _____ for his hard work, the salesperson was promoted to manager.
   (A) fee   (B) reward   (C) percentage   (D) revenue

3. One _____ to living in a small town is there are few entertainment choices.
   (A) business   (B) system   (C) economy   (D) drawback

4. The camera uses another company's technology. We had to _____ it from them.
   (A) follow   (B) build   (C) lose   (D) license

5. It's really cold outside. _____, I still want to go hiking.
   (A) Nevertheless   (B) Also   (C) Even   (D) After

6. Good _____ allows many people to learn about your product.
   (A) customer   (B) industry   (C) marketing   (D) opportunity

7. I'm thinking about investing in a fast food _____.
   (A) franchise   (B) revenue   (C) agreement   (D) benefit

8. Many young people want their _____, but they also want to save money by living with their parents.
   (A) economy   (B) model   (C) system   (D) independence

Phrase Building

Write the correct phrase in each blank. (Remember to use the correct word form.)

⬤ tap into   ⬤ from scratch   ⬤ give up   ⬤ to name a few

My mother started this curtain business _____ 25 years ago. In the beginning, all she had was a good idea and a plan for the future. Over time, the company grew through hard work and strong leadership. Also, my mother hired people she met in curtain design classes, _____ a talent pool that others ignored. My mother says she faced some tough times along the way, but she never _____. Now, her company is one of the largest curtain exporters in the country.

Listening Exercise

 Disc 1, Track 11

Listen to the conversation. Then, answer the following questions.

1. (   ) What worries the man about opening his own company?
    (A) It would be expensive.
    (B) It would be boring.
    (C) It would be risky.
    (D) It would be complicated.

2. (   ) What does the woman imply about franchises?
    (A) The owner still must handle a lot of tasks.
    (B) Firing people is the hardest thing to do.
    (C) Getting along with the franchisor isn't easy.
    (D) Advertising isn't important to a franchise.

3. (   ) Who does the woman recommend that the man speak with?
    (A) Her relative
    (B) Her friend
    (C) Her boss
    (D) Her colleague

Listening Activity Disc 1, Track 12

Listen to the report. Then, fill in the information in the chart.

1. Where will the event be held?	
2. How many franchisors will be there?	
3. Name two types of industries with booths.	
4. How many talks will be given each day?	
5. How much does a ticket to the trade fair cost?	

Discussion Questions

1. Some people like to be their own boss. Others prefer working as a regular employee. What's good and bad about each working style?

2. If you had a chance to open a franchise, which one would it be? Why?

3. International franchises are quickly spreading throughout the world. In your opinion, is that a good or bad thing? Why?

Discussion Activity

Working with several classmates, create your own franchise. What kind of franchise will you start? What will be special about it? How will you find franchisees? How much will you charge them? Finally, don't forget to name your franchise!

Example: We are going to open a haircutting franchise, called Style Wave. The best thing about it will be the super low prices....

Pre-Reading Questions

Discuss these questions in pairs.

1. Who is your favorite cartoon character?

2. Do you use your real name on the Internet? If not, what name do you use?

3. Do you collect any toys or dolls?

Consider the Topic

Read each statement. Check if you agree or disagree with it.

	agree	disagree
1. I like chatting with people online.	☐	☐
2. I've met some Internet friends in person.	☐	☐
3. Commercials with cartoon animals are cute.	☐	☐

Reading Passage Disc 1, Track 13

1   Turn on the TV, and you may see a mouse trying to sell you something.
Go into an Internet chatroom, and you may see people using **monsters**
as avatars. We're entering an age where characters **stand in for** us. From
businesses to online identities to toys, character culture is **taking over**.

5   For decades, companies have used characters as mascots. Two famous ones
are Tony the Tiger (from the USA) and the Michelin Man (from France).
Thanks to modern technology, characters like these have grown into walking,
talking spokespeople. We've reached a point where a 3D pig selling us credit
cards is perfectly normal. Maybe it's because there are already too many ads
10 **featuring** real people. Or, it could be that we feel less pressure when sold
something by a cute character.

This shift is also seen in the way we represent ourselves online. On social
networking sites, forums, and chatrooms, few people use photos of
themselves as avatars. They are more likely to use images of things they like
15 and relate to. Cartoon and movie characters are two popular types.

Interestingly, when we see someone using a Snoopy or Mickey Mouse avatar,
that becomes the way we imagine the person. Internet friends often
comment that it's **strange** to meet in person. They're used to
referring to each other by Internet nicknames and imagining
20 people as their avatars. It's a good example of the "virtual"
world becoming just as important as the "real world."

Connected to these trends is the growth of character toys.
They're collected by children as well as adults. Popular ones
include characters from comic books, cartoons, and video
25 games. Then there are toys based on **original** characters **created**
by artists. These "designer toys" are sold everywhere from
convenience stores to clothing shops. You can even have a toy of
yourself made. Using several photographs, a **specialty** company
can quickly turn you into a 3D figure!

---

3 avatar – picture that represents a person online   20 virtual – made by computers
5 mascot – character that represents a company, team, etc.
8 spokesperson – person who speaks for a company

30   We're becoming **comfortable** with the idea of listening to, speaking with, and even becoming characters. The next generation of online communities may take this a step further. Instead of 2D avatars, we may have 3D characters standing in for us. We're also likely to see more farm animals and cute monsters selling us things. And, of course, there will always be

35   new toys. As character culture grows, the line between the real world and virtual world will continue to blur.

36 blur – become unclear

Questions about the Reading   Choose the best answer.

1. (   ) What is the main idea?
    (A) Toys based on characters are fun to collect.
    (B) Tony the Tiger is a famous mascot.
    (C) Characters have become a part of our daily lives.
    (D) Many people love to watch cartoons.

2. (   ) What does the article suggest about company mascots?
    (A) They rarely act as spokespeople.
    (B) They make customers feel pressured.
    (C) They have been around a long time.
    (D) They are usually based on farm animals.

3. (   ) What type of character toys are NOT mentioned?
    (A) Cartoon characters
    (B) Video game characters
    (C) Movie characters
    (D) Comic book characters

4. (   ) What do you need if you want a toy of yourself made?
    (A) A few photos
    (B) A funny nickname
    (C) A cartoon avatar
    (D) A favorite character

5. (   ) In the future, what may represent people in Internet communities?
    (A) Funny voices
    (B) 3D characters
    (C) Simple pictures
    (D) 2D photos

Writing about the Article
Answer each question based on the article.

1. What country is the Michelin Man from?

_____

2. On the Internet, what are two popular kinds of avatars?

_____

3. What are designer toys?

_____

Vocabulary Building
Choose the best word to fill in each blank.

1. The sofa was so _____, I almost fell asleep sitting on it!
   (A) famous   (B) modern   (C) normal   (D) comfortable

2. In the horror movie, there was a green _____ that ate people.
   (A) technology   (B) monster   (C) shift   (D) nickname

3. The new factory will _____ 300 new jobs for the town.
   (A) imagine   (B) create   (C) continue   (D) relate

4. I _____ on your YouTube video. Did you read what I wrote?
   (A) identified   (B) collected   (C) commented   (D) listened

5. It's a(n) _____ painting by one of the 17th century masters. It's worth a lot of money.
   (A) quick   (B) modern   (C) social   (D) original

6. The dessert shop's _____ is chocolate cake. People come from far away to have a piece.
   (A) specialty   (B) pressure   (C) character   (D) site

7. That's a really _____ dress. I can't imagine anybody wearing it in public!
   (A) cute   (B) normal   (C) strange   (D) perfect

8. The club _____ live music from some of the city's hottest bands.
   (A) grows   (B) stands   (C) enters   (D) features

Phrase Building Write the correct phrase in each blank.

● instead of   ● stand in for   ● take over   ● refer to

There are several small ice cream shops in this city, including one run by my family. Some of us are worried that a giant dessert shop opening in the new mall will try to _____ the market. Rather than sit around and do nothing, I'm driving to New York to get advice from my Uncle Joe. He's a famous businessperson, so we all _____ him as Big Joe. Anyway, while I'm away, my cousin Louie will _____ me at the shop. Hopefully, Big Joe can tell me what to do.

Listening Exercise   Disc 1, Track 14

Listen to the conversation. Then, answer the following questions.

1. (   ) How can people get a free doll?
    (A) By spending money at a store
    (B) By applying for a credit card
    (C) By visiting a website
    (D) By opening an account

2. (   ) What kind of animal is Loony?
    (A) A pig
    (B) A rabbit
    (C) A duck
    (D) A bird

3. (   ) How much does an account need in it to avoid a monthly fee?
    (A) $5
    (B) $35
    (C) $200
    (D) $1,000

Listening Activity Disc 1, Track 15

Listen to the report. Then, fill in the information in the chart.

1. What is the man changing his name to?	
2. Where does the name come from?	
3. How long has he used that name online?	
4. How many websites has the man registered at?	
5. When will he make the name change?	

Discussion Questions

1. Are advertisements with characters in them more successful when targeting children or adults? Or, is it about the same?

2. Let's say you're planning to meet some Internet friends in person. Will you probably use their online nicknames or their real names? Why?

3. On the Net, it's easy for people to hide behind avatars and nicknames. They can behave any way they want. In your opinion, do many people act differently online from the way they act in person?

Discussion Activity

Working in small groups, invent a company mascot. It can be a real company, or you can make the company up. Will the mascot be an animal, robot, or something else? What will its name be? If possible, take out a piece of paper and draw your mascot.

Example: Our mascot, which is for a computer company, is a machine monster. Its head is a computer monitor....

Changes
NEXT EXIT ↗

Pre-Reading Questions

Discuss these questions in pairs.

1. What foreign languages have you studied?

2. What is the hardest thing about studying another language?

3. Is your language pronounced differently by people living in different areas? Can you think of an example?

Consider the Topic

Read each statement. Check if you agree or disagree with it.

	agree	disagree
1. In my native language, young people invent new slang all the time.	☐	☐
2. My language has changed a lot over the last 100 years.	☐	☐
3. It's hard for me to understand the pronunciation of some native English speakers.	☐	☐

Reading Passage Disc 1, Track 16

1   One of the interesting things about languages is the way they change over time. In English, everything from spelling to vocabulary has gone through major changes over the years. In fact, to a modern speaker, the English of 1,000 years ago looks like a foreign language!

5   The history of English **dates back** around 1,500 years. At that time, groups of Europeans **invaded** England, bringing their language with them. It developed into Old English. Later, in 1066, England was invaded by the Normans, from France. The language went through an important shift, leading to what we now call Middle English. Over the next 500 years, the language underwent

10   further shifts, leading to Modern English. As the language has developed over time, many things about it have changed.

Pronunciation is one of the most **obvious** areas. For example, in Old English, people said "hus" and "mus." Now, we say "house" and "mouse."

15   These days, there are many differences in the way English is pronounced in the USA, India, and elsewhere. When people live in groups **separated** by great **distances**, the pace of change can be fast!

Spelling has also gone through interesting changes. For example, in Old

20   English, one wrote "riht." A "g" was added in Middle English, making the spelling "right." Also, in the distant past, people did not always follow **standards** of spelling. In the 18th and 19th centuries, scholars like Noah Webster wrote dictionaries which made the spelling more **consistent**. However, different standards were **decided on** in England and the USA. So,

25   some differences remain – for example, "color" vs. "colour."

Vocabulary changes happen even more quickly. English has grown by borrowing words from languages such as French, Spanish, and Arabic, to name a few. This often happens with types of food – for example, "tofu." Then there is slang, which enters and leaves the language every year! Thirty

---

9 undergo – go through; experience
18 pace – speed

22 scholar – someone who carefully studies something

30 years ago, one often heard people saying "groovy," meaning "great." These days, you'll rarely hear the word, except on old TV shows and movies.

Because English is spoken by so many people worldwide, it really is an exciting time for the language. **Just as** American and British **versions** are always changing, so are versions spoken in Canada, Singapore,
35 and elsewhere. At the same time, an entirely new version of English is appearing on the Internet, with whole new slang and writing styles. In a way, learning English is a never-ending process, even for native speakers!

Questions about the Reading   Choose the best answer.

1. (   ) Around how long ago did the Middle English period begin?
   (A) 500 years
   (B) 1,000 years
   (C) 1,500 years
   (D) 2,000 years

2. (   ) What is the word "riht" an example of?
   (A) A word we no longer use
   (B) A slang term that was once popular
   (C) A new way of pronouncing something
   (D) An old way of spelling a word

3. (   ) What area of language change is NOT mentioned in the article?
   (A) Grammar
   (B) Spelling
   (C) Pronunciation
   (D) Vocabulary

4. (   ) Which of the following is true?
   (A) English does not include any words from Arabic.
   (B) Without training, an American could not understand Old English.
   (C) The word "house" was pronounced the same way 1,500 years ago.
   (D) Standards of spelling are the same in every country.

5. (   ) What does the phrase *to name a few* in line 28 mean?
   (A) among others
   (B) not considering
   (C) around the world
   (D) more or less

Writing about the Article
Answer each question based on the article.

1. When did scholars work on making English spelling more consistent?

_____

2. What are some languages that English has borrowed words from?

_____

3. Where are we seeing an entirely new version of English?

_____

Vocabulary Building
Choose the best word to fill in each blank.

1. What's the _____ from London to Paris?
   (A) shift   (B) distance   (C) process   (D) spelling

2. Which iPod _____ did you get? Mine is one of the first ones.
   (A) slang   (B) difference   (C) history   (D) version

3. What's the _____ of that word? I know what it means, but I don't know how to say it.
   (A) vocabulary   (B) grammar   (C) language   (D) pronunciation

4. Restaurants are careful about keeping the taste of their dishes _____. Customers like to know what they're getting when ordering something.
   (A) consistent   (B) major   (C) important   (D) recent

5. _____ the CDs into two piles – one for yours and one for mine.
   (A) Add   (B) Remain   (C) Separate   (D) Grow

6. An army has clear _____ of behavior. Soldiers must act a certain way and follow orders.
   (A) dictionaries   (B) standards   (C) paces   (D) speakers

7. In a war, one country _____ another.
   (A) borrows   (B) appears   (C) invades   (D) develops

8. The answer to the question was _____. Every student got it right.
   (A) distant   (B) modern   (C) obvious   (D) exciting

Phrase Building

Write the correct phrase in each blank. (Remember to use the correct word form.)

● date back   ● just as   ● go through   ● decide on

My dad and I love books. _____ my father is a lifelong book collector, so am I. Of course, his collection is much larger than mine! My favorite is an old book from Russia. It _____ to 1835. I don't read Russian, but I can appreciate its paper, binding, and beautiful pictures. I'm actually planning to open a shop of my own. I asked my father to help me _____ a shop name. It will either be "Jamal's Book Corner" or "Page after Page."

Listening Exercise

 Disc 1, Track 17

Listen to the conversation. Then, answer the following questions.

1. (   ) How did the man feel about the movie he watched?
   - (A) It was hard to understand.
   - (B) It was really funny.
   - (C) It was a little confusing.
   - (D) It was very modern.

2. (   ) What does the woman do when she doesn't understand a French movie?
   - (A) She stops the film at that point.
   - (B) She replays the movie.
   - (C) She slows the film down.
   - (D) She photographs the screen.

3. (   ) What does the man recommend doing?
   - (A) Learning as much slang as possible
   - (B) Going to the movies on a date
   - (C) Being careful about watching old movies
   - (D) Renting at least 10 different DVDs

Listening Activity Disc 1, Track 18

Listen to the report. Then, fill in the information in the chart.

1. How often is a winner chosen?	
2. When was "carbon neutral" a top winner?	
3. What are winners chosen for?	
4. What is announced besides the top winner?	
5. Why is it becoming hard to choose a winner?	

Discussion Questions

1. Has your language borrowed a lot of words from other languages? Can you think of any examples?

2. The Internet is affecting many languages. What about your language? Do people communicate differently online than in person?

3. Some countries have groups that try to control or stop language change. What's your opinion about that? Is it a good idea? Is it possible?

Discussion Activity

People are always looking for ways to improve their English. Here's a chance for everyone in the class to share ideas. Think of two or three things that work really well for you. Then, share them with the class.

Example: I try to learn a new word every day. In the morning, I write a note on my cell phone. It contains the word, meaning, and example sentence. When I'm on the subway or bus, I read the note....

Pre-Reading Questions

Discuss these questions in pairs.

1. Are you a sports fan? Which sports do you like?

2. What does it take to be a great athlete? (Ex: speed)

3. Have you ever watched Michael Jordan, Tiger Woods, or Alex Rodriguez play on TV?

Consider the Topic

Read each statement. Check if you agree or disagree with it.

	agree	disagree
1. I try to be the best at whatever I do.	☐	☐
2. In my life, I have big goals that I want to reach.	☐	☐
3. When playing a sport, having fun is more important than winning.	☐	☐

Reading Passage Disc 1, Track 19

1   In most professional sports, one or two players come along each generation to **dominate** the game. They break records and set standards of excellence. What is it that **sets them apart**? Besides talent, they must have focus, **confidence**, and a hunger to win. Michael Jordan, Tiger Woods, and Alex
5   Rodriguez are three such athletes. They have given their all in their **pursuit** of perfection.

Michael Jordan was a basketball player with a drive to be the best. From 1984-1993, he led his team to three NBA championships. Then, looking for a new challenge, he switched to playing baseball. In 1995, Jordan went back
10   to the NBA, dominating again and winning three more championships. He retired for the second time in 1999, after a **terrific** career. But his competitive fire still burned. So, in 2001 he came out of retirement yet again and played two more seasons. Even at 40 years of age, Jordan was able to score 40 points in a game!

15   Tiger Woods also seems like he was born to win. At just nine months of age, Woods picked up a golf club and copied his father's swing. As a young boy, he appeared on TV shows and magazine covers. Also, as if preparing for the future, he taped a copy of Jack
20   Nicklaus's golf records on his wall. Tiger's focus has driven him to win many tournaments, first as an **amateur** and then as a professional. He is **closing in on** Nicklaus's record of 18 major championships. Though the spotlight is always on him, Tiger ignores
25   the pressure, maintains focus, and keeps on winning.

Baseball, another sport rich in heroes, has had few as talented as Alex Rodriguez. During A-Rod's career, he has dealt with incredible pressure from fans and the media. Because of his high salary, they have expected him to play like a superman. For his part, he has delivered, year after year. In 2007,
30   A-Rod became the youngest player ever to hit 500 home runs. **Odds are** he

---

⁴ hunger – desire
⁹ switch – change
¹¹ competitive – with a strong desire to win

²¹ tournament – competition
²⁴ spotlight – focused attention
²⁴ ignore – pay no attention to

31 will break many more records before retiring. As his hero, Cal Ripken, said about him, "He has talent that **flows** with every action."

When a special athlete comes along, he or she has a big **impact** on a sport. Jordan, Woods, and Rodriguez have all made their sport more popular.
35 Plus, like all great players, they have pushed others to **perform** at a higher level. Their talent, focus, and hard work force other athletes to step up or step aside.

[36] step up – perform at a higher level   [37] step aside – move out of the way

Questions about the Reading   Choose the best answer.

1. (   ) What is the main idea?
    (A) Michael Jordan was the greatest basketball player ever.
    (B) Excellent athletes almost never lose.
    (C) Breaking records is the mark of success.
    (D) It takes several special qualities to be a top athlete.

2. (   ) When did Michael Jordan switch from basketball to baseball?
    (A) 1984
    (B) 1993
    (C) 1995
    (D) 1999

3. (   ) What does the article imply about Jack Nicklaus?
    (A) He was Tiger's golf teacher.
    (B) He was a great golf player.
    (C) He only won a few tournaments.
    (D) He has some unbreakable records.

4. (   ) How has Tiger Woods succeeded in the face of so much pressure?
    (A) By learning to ignore the pressure
    (B) By putting the spotlight on others
    (C) By hiring great coaches
    (D) By winning once in a while

5. (   ) What is true about Alex Rodriguez?
    (A) All fans support him, no matter what he does.
    (B) His worst year playing was in 2007.
    (C) A-Rod's success has come at a very young age.
    (D) He is Cal Ripken's hero.

Writing about the Article
Answer each question based on the article.

1. In total, how many championships did Michael Jordan win?

_____

2. What did Tiger Woods tape on his wall when he was young?

_____

3. How do great athletes affect other players?

_____

Vocabulary Building
Choose the best word to fill in each blank.

1. The movie is _____. I would highly recommend it.
   (A) competitive   (B) terrific   (C) rich   (D) high

2. We just hired an excellent new salesperson. We think he'll have a big _____ on our sales numbers.
   (A) generation   (B) standard   (C) perfection   (D) impact

3. This river _____ across the valley and empties into the ocean.
   (A) flows   (B) sets   (C) keeps   (D) burns

4. I love playing chess, but I'm just a(n) _____. You'll easily beat me.
   (A) amateur   (B) future   (C) talent   (D) focus

5. If you have _____, other people will also believe in you.
   (A) action   (B) challenge   (C) season   (D) confidence

6. When it comes to office software, Microsoft has _____ the market for more than a decade.
   (A) switched   (B) dominated   (C) maintained   (D) prepared

7. The equipment isn't _____ as it should. It may need to be repaired.
   (A) expecting   (B) retiring   (C) ignoring   (D) performing

8. Sally wants to be the best violinist in her school. Nothing is more important to her than the _____ of that goal.
   (A) salary   (B) athlete   (C) pursuit   (D) talent

Phrase Building

Write the correct phrase in each blank. (Remember to use the correct word form.)

● set someone apart   ● close in on   ● come along   ● odds are

Kaho is the best salesperson we've ever had. I think her winning attitude is what _____ from everyone else. Every time she speaks with a customer, she believes she'll close the deal. Kaho has already sold 336 houses, and she's quickly _____ our all-time record. That's amazing, as our company has been around for 30 years. _____ she'll break the record some time this year. If she does, she'll receive a big bonus and may be made into a full partner.

Listening Exercise

 Disc 1, Track 20

Listen to the conversation. Then, answer the following questions.

1. (   ) What surprises the woman about Alex Rodriguez?
    (A) His behavior
    (B) His salary
    (C) His playing
    (D) His record

2. (   ) How does the man feel about the woman's opinion?
    (A) He agrees with it.
    (B) He thinks she's partly right.
    (C) He finds it confusing.
    (D) He has a different opinion.

3. (   ) What baseball income source is NOT mentioned by the man?
    (A) Clothing
    (B) Video games
    (C) Tickets
    (D) Television deals

Listening Activity Disc 1, Track 21

Listen to the report. Then, fill in the information in the chart.

1. What are some people saying Michael Jordan wants to do?	
2. Around how old is he?	
3. How does Jordan look?	
4. What may be Jordan's biggest problem?	
5. What is suggested about the reports?	

Discussion Questions

1. Before Tiger Woods came along, golf wasn't such a popular sport on TV. Now, millions of people watch golf when he plays. How about you?

2. When superstar athletes like Michael Jordan play, they sometimes dominate the sport for years. In your opinion, is that fair to other athletes? Why or why not?

3. Does everyone have a chance to be the best at what they do? Or, are some people born with talents that make it easier for them to succeed?

Discussion Activity

Hold a mini debate. On one side are two or three classmates who think athletes are overpaid. On the other side are two or three classmates who think athletes deserve their high salaries. First, each side should spend a few minutes thinking of reasons for its point of view. Then, hold the mini debate.

Example: We think athletes are overpaid. If they didn't earn so much, teams could lower ticket prices....

Bicycling around Taiwan 8

Pre-Reading Questions
Discuss these questions in pairs.

1. Do you prefer to walk, ride a bike, drive a car, or ride a motorcycle?

2. Have you ever taken a trip with a group of classmates or colleagues?

3. What are some great places in your country to travel to?

Consider the Topic
Read each statement. Check if you agree or disagree with it.

	agree	disagree
1. I would love to go on a long bike trip.	☐	☐
2. It can be dangerous to ride a bike on the street.	☐	☐
3. I try to spend as little money as possible during trips.	☐	☐

Reading Passage Disc 1, Track 22

1   Taiwan is one of Asia's most beautiful countries. With a lovely coastline and tall, proud mountains, the island is a feast for **nature** lovers. At the same time, Taiwan has an **extensive** road system, making it easy to travel from place to place. All this has helped make local tourism popular. In increasing numbers,

5   people are making trips around Taiwan via bicycle. It's a fun and interesting way to **explore** the island.

   Proper planning is key. For a bike trip covering some 700 kilometers, several weeks of **training** are needed. Having the right equipment is also important. Experienced travelers recommend a bike that can change gears. That's helpful

10   when going up and down mountain roads. A bike **repair** kit is also necessary, as is proper clothing. Above all, one should pack lightly, keeping the total weight less than five kilograms.

   Many travelers make the trip alone. Others go with colleagues, classmates, or people they meet online.

15   Usually, there are between 3 and 10 people in a group. Students with **time on their hands typically** take 10-15 days to circle the island. People with full-time jobs usually take shorter trips of 7-9 days. In general, the summer months, with their warmer weather, work best

20   for a trip. However, travelers need to check weather reports to make sure no typhoons are on the way.

   During the trip, bikers **stick to** county roads since they may not travel on highways. In the north and east, the coastline offers excellent views. In the south, Kenting is a well-loved area with great beaches.

25   And, in the west, many bikers **stop off** in Kaohsiung, Tainan, Taichung, and other interesting cities. Some travelers leave their bikes in Chiayi and take a bus up to Alishan.

   For many people, a key point is traveling as cheaply as possible. Careful spenders can make the trip on just 5,000 NT! Of course, that means sleeping in

---

2 feast – large amount of something good
7 kilometer – 1 kilometer equals 0.62 miles
10 gear – switch that lets you change speeds on a bike
11 proper – suitable
29 NT – New Taiwan dollar (the currency of Taiwan)

30 very cheap places, including, possibly, several nights spent outdoors. Meals
are also basic, with convenience stores serving as popular eating spots.

To keep safe, people should wear a helmet and special clothing that makes
it easy for cars to see them. Also, there are stretches of road (such as the
SuHao Public Road) which can be dangerous. Yet, as long as one prepares
35 well and is careful, problems can be kept to a **minimum**. Kilometer
after kilometer, travelers can enjoy the freedom of the open road while
experiencing Taiwan's rich natural beauty.

33 stretches – lengths

Questions about the Reading   Choose the best answer.

1. (   ) What do most people do before bicycling around Taiwan?
    (A) Save up a lot of money
    (B) Buy a very cheap bicycle
    (C) Train for a few weeks
    (D) Bicycle exactly 700 kilometers

2. (   ) Which of the following pieces of equipment is NOT recommended?
    (A) Repair kit
    (B) Suitable clothes
    (C) Dark sunglasses
    (D) Gear changing bike

3. (   ) How long do office workers usually spend on the trip?
    (A) 1-5 days
    (B) 3-10 days
    (C) 7-9 days
    (D) 10-15 days

4. (   ) According to the article, what do travelers to Alishan do with their bikes?
    (A) They load them onto the bus to Alishan.
    (B) They ride them to Alishan.
    (C) They find a place to store them in Chiayi.
    (D) They ship them home.

5. (   ) Which of the following is true about bike trips around Taiwan?
    (A) Bicyclists can travel on any road they want.
    (B) Helmets only need to be worn on the SuHao Public Road.
    (C) It is possible to spend just 5,000 NT on the trip.
    (D) Students usually take shorter trips than full-time workers.

Writing about the Article
Answer each question based on the article.

1. When is it helpful to have a bicycle that can change gears?

_____

2. What time of year is usually best for a long bike trip?

_____

3. What is a highlight of traveling through northern and eastern Taiwan?

_____

Vocabulary Building
Choose the best word to fill in each blank.

1. I brought the broken camera back to the shop, and they _____ it in less than a week.
   (A) recommended (B) repaired (C) covered (D) experienced

2. Since it's late, let's try to keep the noise to a _____.
   (A) view (B) kilometer (C) point (D) minimum

3. The city has _____ subway and bus systems. You can go anywhere using public transportation.
   (A) dangerous (B) basic (C) careful (D) extensive

4. New employees go through two weeks of _____ to learn about the job.
   (A) clothing (B) packing (C) training (D) circling

5. _____, 100-150 people attend each concert.
   (A) Typically (B) Helpfully (C) Lightly (D) Shortly

6. People who live in cities often go to parks to be closer to _____.
   (A) system (B) nature (C) weight (D) equipment

7. I've only lived in this neighborhood a few days, so I haven't had a chance to _____ the area.
   (A) explore (B) wear (C) require (D) serve

8. It gets very cold at night, so remember to wear _____ clothing.
   (A) natural (B) important (C) cheap (D) proper

Phrase Building Write the correct phrase in each blank. (Remember to use the correct word form.)

● on the way ● time on one's hands ● stick to ● stop off

Last year, several friends and I traveled across Europe by train. Our route took us from France to Greece. Besides visiting some big cities, we _____ in several small towns. During most of the trip, we _____ the plan that we had made beforehand. However, one day, we missed our train! The next one didn't come for another 12 hours, so we had extra _____. We walked around, had lunch, and wrote postcards. It was one of my favorite days of the trip!

Listening Exercise Disc 1, Track 23

Listen to the conversation. Then, answer the following questions.

1. (   ) Why does the man want to go to Alishan?
   (A) It's not far from his home.
   (B) Few people travel there.
   (C) He would like to see snow.
   (D) A friend recommended it.

2. (   ) Where do the people probably live?
   (A) Ilan
   (B) Taitung
   (C) Kenting
   (D) Keelung

3. (   ) What does the man suggest doing?
   (A) Buying a travel guide
   (B) Reserving train tickets
   (C) Asking for time off work
   (D) Deciding who to travel with

Listening Activity Disc 1, Track 24

Listen to the advertisement. Then, fill in the information in the chart.

1. What vacation spot is the discount for?	
2. How much does the Super Green package cost?	
3. How many nights are included?	
4. How much does an additional night cost?	
5. How much can people save by traveling in a group?	

Discussion Questions

1. What do you like to do when you travel somewhere? (Relax? Shop? Eat? Everything?)

2. Do you have any interesting or funny stories from a trip that you've taken? If so, tell one. If not, talk about a place that you've visited in the last year or two.

3. If you could travel to any place in the world, where would you go?

Discussion Activity

Working with three or four classmates, plan a trip around your country! How long will your trip be? Where will you go? How will you get from place to place? If possible, draw a map. When you're done, share your plan with the rest of the class.

Example: We're going to spend two weeks traveling around Brazil. We'll start in São Paulo and will get around by bus and train....

The End of Privacy 9

Pre-Reading Questions
Discuss these questions in pairs.

1. What personal information do stores ask for when you apply for a store membership card? (Ex: birth date)

2. Are you a very private person? In other words, do you mind if other people know details about your life?

3. Do you carry your cell phone with you all the time?

Consider the Topic

Read each statement. Check if you agree or disagree with it.

	agree	disagree
1. There are a lot of security cameras in my city.	☐	☐
2. I'm worried about identity theft.	☐	☐
3. The more information the government has about us, the better it can protect us.	☐	☐

Reading Passage Disc 1, Track 25

1   People used to say that everyone wanted their 15 minutes of fame. These days, the saying goes that people are worried about having 15 minutes of privacy. Details about our lives, from Internet purchases to walks in the park, are more public than ever. In some ways, **data gathering** and video
5   surveillance are turning our lives into open books.

Without question, we live in an information age. When applying for credit cards or visiting a doctor, our personal data is passed from person to person. Unfortunately, that information isn't always safely stored. Identity theft is widespread, as are database thefts. According to one **estimate**, more
10   than 160 million personal records were stolen in 2007. That was more than four times the 2006 amount.

Then there's the Internet. E-tailers, social networking sites, and other sites often **track** our online activity. Google has **come under fire** more than any other company. Through its search engine, Gmail, and tools like the Google
15   Toolbar, the company can record many of your moves. That may include searches made, websites visited, and items **purchased**. **Critics** say this is a serious privacy risk. Google says the data is safe, and the company only uses it to improve our online experiences.

These days, our privacy is even at **risk** when we
20   go outside. **Security** cameras are attached to street lamps, traffic lights, and buildings. Satellites high above the Earth also look down on us. Supporters say we live in dangerous times, and surveillance makes us safer. Critics say it **chips away at** our
25   freedom. Whoever's right, the surveillance industry is red hot, worth an estimated $10 billion in 2008.

When we travel from place to place, our privacy is also affected. Cell phones can be tracked, letting people with the right equipment know our location. ID cards and passports are starting to use computer chips that store

---

⁵ surveillance – closely watching a person or place
¹² e-tailer – online shop
¹² social networking site – website where people meet, chat, etc.
²¹ satellite – machine circling the Earth (or other planet) in space

30   personal information. Also, more countries are starting to fingerprint and photograph foreign visitors. Again, that's done for security reasons.

     As our privacy disappears **bit by bit**, some people are trying to live as simply as possible. By staying offline and limiting the flow of personal data, they're trying to "fly under the radar." Others are actually embracing

35   the situation. They accept that they are "public figures" and look for ways to turn it to their advantage. To millions of bloggers and other online celebrities, the idea of privacy is a thing of the past.

34 fly under the radar – avoid attention   34 embrace – welcome

Questions about the Reading   **Choose the best answer.**

1. (   ) What is the main idea?
   - (A) People have much less privacy than they used to.
   - (B) Few people are worried about their privacy.
   - (C) Keeping any information private is impossible.
   - (D) Our privacy is at risk when we go outside.

2. (   ) What year were some 160 million personal records stolen?
   - (A) 2005
   - (B) 2006
   - (C) 2007
   - (D) 2008

3. (   ) What concerns people about Google?
   - (A) The usefulness of its software
   - (B) The quality of visits to the site
   - (C) The amount of data it collects
   - (D) The speed of Google searches

4. (   ) What does the article suggest about the surveillance industry?
   - (A) The industry is growing at a fast rate.
   - (B) It may fall in value to $10 billion in 2008.
   - (C) Office buildings are its biggest clients.
   - (D) Its supporters worry about our freedom.

5. (   ) According to the article, what makes it easy to figure out our location?
   - (A) Passports
   - (B) The Google Toolbar
   - (C) Credit cards
   - (D) Cell phones

Writing about the Article

Answer each question based on the article.

1. What are two types of websites that often track our online activity?

_____

2. Where are many security cameras placed?

_____

3. What are some people doing to protect their privacy?

_____

Vocabulary Building

Choose the best word to fill in each blank.

1. During the prime minister's visit, _____ at the airport was very high.
   (A) privacy   (B) information   (C) security   (D) industry

2. We carefully study our sales _____ to look for ways to increase profits.
   (A) data   (B) fame   (C) theft   (D) equipment

3. I'd like to _____ the motorcycle, but I don't have enough money.
   (A) record   (B) search   (C) travel   (D) purchase

4. We _____ the cost will be $10 per unit, though that could go up.
   (A) attach   (B) estimate   (C) affect   (D) disappear

5. There are a few _____ of the plan, but most people support it.
   (A) figures   (B) critics   (C) ideas   (D) celebrities

6. Before you open a business, you should _____ as much information as you can about the field.
   (A) gather   (B) limit   (C) affect   (D) visit

7. Using modern technology, pet owners can _____ their pets' movements. That's helpful in case an animal gets lost.
   (A) apply   (B) pass   (C) worry   (D) track

8. When playing a sport, there's always a _____ of getting hurt.
   (A) detail   (B) tool   (C) risk   (D) search

Phrase Building

Write the correct phrase in each blank. (Remember to use the correct word form.)

● come under fire   ● chip away at   ● regardless of   ● bit by bit

The last few years have been hard for our firm. Competitors are _____ our market share, and profits are falling. Everyone is nervous, and the sales managers have really _____. They're being pressured by our director to increase sales. That might be possible by building a new website and expanding overseas. If we can do that, the situation should improve _____. However, it will take time to reach a top position in the field again.

Listening Exercise

 Disc 1, Track 26

Listen to the conversation. Then, answer the following questions.

1. (   ) What does the woman collect?
    (A) Statues
    (B) Jewelry
    (C) Vases
    (D) Plates

2. (   ) What surprised the woman?
    (A) The website's membership fees
    (B) The limited content on the site
    (C) The minimum age requirement
    (D) The type of information requested

3. (   ) What did the woman do?
    (A) She registered for the forums.
    (B) She found another website.
    (C) She decided to leave the site.
    (D) She wrote an e-mail to the site owner.

Listening Activity Disc 1, Track 27

Listen to the report. Then, fill in the information in the chart.

1. What time did the crime take place?	
2. What kind of store was robbed?	
3. What did the computer system tell the police?	
4. After being alerted by the system, how long did it take the police catch the thief?	
5. Where was the thief caught?	

Discussion Questions

1. Do the increasing number of security cameras bother you? Or, do they give you an added feeling of safety?

2. Do you feel people have more freedom than they used to, or less? Why?

3. More countries are taking travelers' fingerprints and photographs at the border. How do you feel about that?

Discussion Activity

Hold a mini debate. On one side are several people who think safety is more important than freedom. On the other side are several people with the opposite opinion. They think privacy and freedom are more important than anything else. First, spend several minutes deciding on reasons for your side's point of view. Then, hold the mini debate.

Example: We think safety is more important than freedom. If you don't do anything wrong, then you don't need to worry about the government knowing all about you....

Pre-Reading Questions

Discuss these questions in pairs.

1. What are some causes of global warming?

2. How can a city lower its air pollution levels?

3. Who bears the most responsibility for helping the environment: the government, businesses, or ordinary people?

Consider the Topic

Read each statement. Check if you agree or disagree with it.

	agree	disagree
1. Every person shares some of the blame for global warming.	☐	☐
2. I would be willing to donate money to help the environment.	☐	☐
3. If we work together, we can solve any problem.	☐	☐

Reading Passage Disc 1, Track 28

1   The threat caused by global climate change is **familiar** to us all. Every day, we burn fossil fuels like coal and oil for energy. That **releases** tons of CO_2 into the air, leading to global warming. One way people, businesses, and governments are meeting the threat is by going carbon neutral. The idea is to

5   release a net balance of zero CO_2. If enough people **get involved**, it can have a real impact in the fight against global warming.

Many of our daily activities **produce** CO_2. Driving, flying, using computers, and heating our homes all add to the problem. "Carbon calculators" can show you how much CO_2 you are **responsible for**. For example, flying from

10   San Francisco to Tokyo releases almost one ton of CO_2 per person. And, driving 20 kilometers to work produces around two tons per year.

Once you know how much CO_2 you produce, you can start lowering your "carbon footprint." That can be done

15   by buying energy-**efficient** light bulbs, refrigerators, and other appliances. By **installing** solar panels, we can make homes and businesses greener. Also, walking, riding bicycles, and driving

20   hybrid cars all help reduce CO_2 levels.

Even after taking steps to save energy, we still create some pollution. So, the next step in going carbon neutral is to "offset" that amount. Offsetting means supporting energy-saving efforts that balance out the CO_2 that you produce. Some examples are tree planting groups, solar energy **projects**, and other

25   clean energy efforts. So, let's say your **lifestyle** produces 30 tons of CO_2. You could offset that total by giving money to a wind farm to produce 30 tons of clean energy. The net balance is zero.

Efforts to go carbon neutral are **showing up** everywhere. For example, the Olympics is now a carbon neutral event. So are entire schools, such as the

---

¹ climate – general weather
² coal – black rock burned for fuel/heat
² CO₂ – carbon dioxide

⁵ net – total/final
¹⁴ footprint – amount produced
¹⁶ appliance – electrical device (Ex: stove)

30 College of the Atlantic. Bands like the Rolling Stones are releasing carbon neutral CDs. And, some people are even offsetting their weddings!

We're facing a real urgency with the climate crisis. Many scientists say we need to lower CO_2 levels by 60% over the next 40 years. If we don't, there could be terrible **consequences**, both for the environment and the world
35 economy. Though governments are talking about ways to lower pollution levels, they may not be enough. By going carbon neutral, people and businesses can really do something to meet this global challenge.

[32] urgency – need to act quickly

Questions about the Reading   Choose the best answer.

1. (   ) What can help people figure out their CO_2 production?
    (A) Energy-efficient light bulbs
    (B) A carbon calculator
    (C) Solar panels for your home
    (D) Coal or another fuel

2. (   ) About how much CO_2 is produced by a flight across the Pacific Ocean?
    (A) 1 ton per person
    (B) 2 tons per person
    (C) 20 tons per person
    (D) 30 tons per person

3. (   ) What would NOT help you lower your carbon footprint?
    (A) Taking more airplane rides
    (B) Using appliances that use less energy
    (C) Riding a bicycle to and from work
    (D) Buying a hybrid car

4. (   ) How might you offset the pollution produced by driving to work?
    (A) By driving your car more often
    (B) By donating to a solar energy farm
    (C) By reading about energy-efficient refrigerators
    (D) By producing two tons of CO_2

5. (   ) What does the article imply?
    (A) A CO_2 drop of 40% by 2050 will solve our climate problems.
    (B) Governments can improve the environment by themselves.
    (C) There aren't any carbon neutral schools, but there will be soon.
    (D) Each of us can help in the fight against global warming.

Writing about the Article

Answer each question based on the article.

1. What is one home appliance that can reduce your carbon footprint?

_____

2. What are some ways to offset the pollution that you create?

_____

3. Which major sporting event is now carbon neutral?

_____

Vocabulary Building

Choose the best word to fill in each blank.

1. I may need help _____ the new hardware. Are you free tomorrow evening?
   (A) meeting   (B) installing   (C) causing   (D) planting

2. Three of us are working on the store redesign _____.
   (A) level   (B) project   (C) energy   (D) total

3. It gets really loud at times. It's a(n) _____ of living near the airport.
   (A) balance   (B) economy   (C) effort   (D) consequence

4. Maria is a very _____ employee. She always finishes her work on time.
   (A) global   (B) entire   (C) terrible   (D) efficient

5. You get to travel a lot and meet famous people. That sounds like a great _____.
   (A) lifestyle   (B) government   (C) crisis   (D) scientist

6. My favorite writer is _____ a new collection of short stories. I'm so excited!
   (A) lowering   (B) facing   (C) releasing   (D) heating

7. The factory _____ tables, chairs, and other furniture.
   (A) produces   (B) supports   (C) burns   (D) reduces

8. I'm not _____ with that store. Has it been open long?
   (A) neutral   (B) sharp   (C) familiar   (D) clean

Phrase Building
Write the correct phrase in each blank. (Remember to use the correct word form.)

● get involved   ● responsible for   ● balance out   ● show up

My older sister and I first _____ with Pacific Tree Planters in 2006. We spend three weekends a month helping the group plant trees. It's actually a lot harder than it sounds. We have to _____ at the office at 6:30 in the morning. After a quick cup of coffee, we load the equipment into the trucks. I'm _____ making sure that it's all properly loaded. Next, we drive to the day's site and spend four hours planting trees. It's important work, but it sure is tiring!

Listening Exercise   Disc 1, Track 29

Listen to the conversation. Then, answer the following questions.

1. (   ) What does the man want to do?
   (A) Donate to charity
   (B) Cut his entertainment costs
   (C) Reduce his carbon output
   (D) Ask for a 15% raise

2. (   ) According to the man, what is the easiest change to make?
   (A) Taking a bus to work
   (B) Living without air conditioning
   (C) Watching fewer movies
   (D) Replacing light bulbs

3. (   ) How many family members will change their lifestyle?
   (A) None of them
   (B) Two of them
   (C) Most of them
   (D) All of them

Listening Activity Disc 1, Track 30

Listen to the report. Then, fill in the information in the chart.

1. Where is the wedding going to take place?	
2. How many people may be seated?	
3. What will guests do after the ceremony?	
4. What are guests asked not to do?	
5. How much are they asked to donate?	

Discussion Questions

1. Think about your daily activities for a moment. Which of them creates the most pollution?

2. Understanding all the environmental issues facing us is not easy. Which issue do you pay the most attention to?

3. Raising taxes could be one way to raise money for the environment. How do you feel about that idea?

Discussion Activity

You and your company just took a trip to New Zealand. Your boss wants to make the trip carbon neutral. He's leaving it up to the staff to decide how. In small groups, discuss what you're going to do. (Will you donate money? Will you join a tree planting group?) After you decide, share your idea with the class.

Example: We want a solution that isn't just a "one-time" payment. So, we will install solar panels on our building's roof....

Pre-Reading Questions

Discuss these questions in pairs.

1. What kinds of storms are common in your country? (Rain? Snow?)

2. What are some causes of air pollution?

3. Have you ever been through a dust storm? Describe the experience.

Consider the Topic

Read each statement. Check if you agree or disagree with it.

	agree	disagree
1. I generally like the weather in my country.	☐	☐
2. I'm frightened by large storms.	☐	☐
3. Air pollution is getting worse every year.	☐	☐

Reading Passage 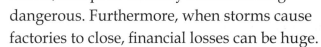 Disc 2, Track 1

1   As China's **remarkable** growth continues, the country faces huge environmental problems. One of the biggest is the yearly dust storms which blow across the country. They **pose a health risk**, cost businesses billions of dollars, and leave parts of the country coated in yellow dust. The problem is so severe it's even

5   affecting China's neighbors as well as countries thousands of kilometers away.

The dust storm season lasts from March to May. Strong winds pick up dirt from the **vast** deserts and plains of northern and northwestern China and Mongolia. The dirt is then carried eastward across China. Along the way, it mixes with air pollution from factories. The **toxic** mix is then dumped on

10 cities like Beijing and Tianjin. The storms then continue on, often affecting Korea, Japan, and Taiwan. In fact, some storms blow all the way across the Pacific Ocean, impacting the USA and Canada.

The storms have a range of consequences. As cities are covered in layers of dust, buildings, streets, and homes must be

15 frequently cleaned. During serious storms, children, **elderly** people, and those with respiratory problems are **advised** to stay indoors. Schools and airports are sometimes closed, and poor visibility makes driving

20 dangerous. Furthermore, when storms cause factories to close, financial losses can be huge.

Dust storms are **nothing new** in China. However, they have become more frequent and serious in recent years. A key reason is the overuse of land. Farmers work the land too **intensively**, weakening the soil. And, China's

25 massive livestock population – around 400 million animals – strips grasslands of their protective covering. In its weakened state, the soil is easily lifted by strong winds. Also, the lack of trees and grass makes it easier for deserts to spread. That, **in turn**, makes the cycle of dust storms even worse.

China is taking steps to tackle this crisis. The top priority is stopping

---

⁴ coated – covered
⁹ dumped on – dropped on
¹² impacting – affecting
¹⁷ respiratory – related to breathing

¹⁹ visibility – the ability to see clearly in an area
²⁵ massive – very large
²⁵ livestock – farm animals
²⁹ tackle – meet; deal with

30 desertification by improving the strength of the soil. Under a government program, which started in 2000, vast areas are being **converted** to grassland and woodland. The goal is to **restore** 205,000 square kilometers of land.

There is a pressing need to solve the problem soon. Millions of people have already been forced from their homes due to the spread of deserts. Many
35 others, from China to Japan and beyond, are suffering from the yearly storms. Meeting the problem is a key test of China's ability to balance economic growth with environmental protection.

³⁰ desertification – the spread of a desert in an area   ³³ pressing – urgent

Questions about the Reading   Choose the best answer.

1. (   ) Where do yellow dust storms begin?
   (A) Northern China and Mongolia
   (B) Many East Asian countries
   (C) Taiwan, Japan, and Korea
   (D) The USA and Canada

2. (   ) How is China planning to stop the storms?
   (A) By preventing overgrazing
   (B) By changing the direction of the wind
   (C) By banning new farms
   (D) By stopping the spread of deserts

3. (   ) What is NOT mentioned as a cause of the storms?
   (A) The small number of trees
   (B) Increasing wind speeds
   (C) The loss of grasslands
   (D) Heavy land use by farmers

4. (   ) What does the word *strips* in line 25 mean?
   (A) buries
   (B) applies
   (C) removes
   (D) covers

5. (   ) Which of the following is an implied consequence of dust storms?
   (A) People are forced to move to the desert.
   (B) New economic opportunities are opened up.
   (C) Travelers cannot fly due to canceled flights.
   (D) Schools have to stay open longer.

Writing about the Article

Answer each question based on the article.

1. When do most dust storms occur?

   _____

2. What types of places are sometimes closed due to dust storms?

   _____

3. How much land does China hope to restore under the government program?

   _____

Vocabulary Building

Choose the best word to fill in each blank.

1. Because he studied _____, he received a good grade on the test.
   (A) eastwardly   (B) yearly   (C) intensively   (D) vastly

2. They repainted the old room to _____ it to its former beauty.
   (A) restore   (B) become   (C) face   (D) cause

3. My history teacher, who is very smart, knows a _____ number of facts about world history.
   (A) remarkable   (B) pressing   (C) poor   (D) toxic

4. Many _____ people have interesting stories of their past experiences.
   (A) severe   (B) elderly   (C) economic   (D) massive

5. Scientists _____ students to eat a good breakfast on the day of an important test.
   (A) affect   (B) continue   (C) remark   (D) advise

6. Pollution is harmful to humans because much of it is _____.
   (A) protective   (B) weakened   (C) financial   (D) toxic

7. Some websites help students _____ kilometers to miles.
   (A) spread   (B) convert   (C) suffer   (D) improve

8. The Gobi Desert is a(n) _____ desert in Asia.
   (A) environmental   (B) vast   (C) intensive   (D) elderly

Phrase Building Write the correct phrase in each blank.

● take steps   ● in turn   ● nothing new   ● pose a health risk

Many forests and grasslands have shrunk, or have even disappeared, in recent decades. So, the idea of restoring them is _____. Scientists have tested many methods of restoring grasslands, often with positive results. Typically, they plant grass in places where it has disappeared. Other projects have even reintroduced animals and plants. _____, these places have been converted to the flourishing states they were once in. Not only does this help plant and animal species, but it also helps prevent the dust storms that _____ to humans.

Listening Exercise   Disc 2, Track 2

Listen to the conversation. Then, answer the following questions.

1. ( ) How does the man feel about today's weather?
    (A) He thinks it's too hot.
    (B) He's unhappy about the wind.
    (C) He's glad it's so warm.
    (D) He's worried it will rain.

2. ( ) What does the woman say about dust storms?
    (A) The dust makes her clothes dirty.
    (B) The dirt damages her car.
    (C) The wind bothers her.
    (D) The storms make her scared.

3. ( ) Why does the man want it to rain tomorrow?
    (A) He enjoys rainy weather.
    (B) It may reduce the dust.
    (C) The temperature will be cooler.
    (D) His car needs to be washed.

65

Listening Activity Disc 2, Track 3

Listen to the report. Then, fill in the information in the chart.

1. What will continue tomorrow?	
2. How many days of dust storms have they had this year?	
3. When did the dust storm season begin?	
4. What will end by Friday?	
5. When will the next weather update be given?	

Discussion Questions

1. What is the most serious weather concern in your country?

2. In your opinion, what should be done to prevent dust storms from reaching your country?

3. Do many grasslands and forests need to be restored in your country? What's the best way to make that happen?

Discussion Activity

Divide into groups of three or four students per group. Each group is going to plan a program to help the environment. First, choose one problem that you want to help solve. Then, decide on three ways to improve the situation. Do you need to ask the government for money? How will you spread your message?

Example: Our team is going to help the wild bear population. We're going to ask the government for money to build new habitats for these beautiful animals....

Pre-Reading Questions

Discuss these questions in pairs.

1. What jobs pay very well?

2. What does a CEO do?

3. Besides a salary, how else do people earn money from a job?
   (Ex: a yearly bonus)

Consider the Topic

Read each statement. Check if you agree or disagree with it.

	agree	disagree
1. I would like to be the head of a large company.	☐	☐
2. CEOs of big companies deserve high salaries.	☐	☐
3. People should not receive money from a company after they are fired.	☐	☐

Reading Passage Disc 2, Track 4

1   Over the past 20 years, the pay packages of the USA's top CEOs have **gone through the roof**. Even when CEOs are fired, they may walk away with millions of dollars. The situation has led to a heated debate in the business world. Just how much does one person deserve to earn?

5   To be fair, a CEO's job is far from easy. As a firm's top executive, he or she has a lot of **responsibility**. The CEO **represents** a company, shapes its direction, and makes **decisions** that affect thousands of

10   workers. In good times and bad, the CEO stands as the face of the company, taking the **credit** or blame for its performance.

A CEO's pay package includes payments such as a salary, stock options, and **bonuses**. In 2005, the average pay package for a CEO of a top US company

15   was $15 million. That was 262 times what the average worker earned. In contrast, in 1965, the average CEO earned 24 times what the average worker brought home. Supporters of today's big pay plans say they're necessary to attract top talent. Critics say many people in a company contribute to its success, not just the top executives.

20   Even when a company is bought, sold, or **merged**, a CEO's financial situation can improve. Their **contracts** often provide "golden parachutes" in case the company changes ownership. When Gillette was bought by Procter & Gamble, Gillette's CEO received a package worth $165 million. After Toys 'R' Us was sold in 2005, the CEO walked away with $63 million, even

25   though the company faced problems.

CEOs can also have big pay days when they retire or are fired. ExxonMobil's CEO, upon retiring, left with an "exit package" worth $400 million. The Home Depot's CEO received $209 million when he left the company in 2007. And that was from a company whose stock price had sharply fallen. The list

---

¹ CEO – Chief Executive Officer
³ heated – passionate
⁶ executive – upper manager

¹³ stock option – chance to buy a stock at a certain price
¹⁸ contribute – add/help out

30   goes on, including some very good, and some very bad, CEOs.

The CEO pay situation has made people **furious**. Shareholders are calling for pay packages to be tied to a company's performance. They also want to see an end to golden parachutes. Indeed, some companies, like Microsoft and Google, do not offer exit packages to executives. Still, **by and large**,

35   a CEO of a large US company can expect to live very comfortably. That usually **holds true** even if the firm's stock value is weak or if the company is bought, sold, or merged.

[32] tied to – connected to

Questions about the Reading   Choose the best answer.

1. ( ) What does the article suggest about CEOs?
    (A) They make far less money than they used to.
    (B) CEOs have jobs which are very difficult.
    (C) They enjoy taking credit but avoid taking blame.
    (D) Most earn more than $15 million yearly.

2. ( ) Which of the following is NOT common in a CEO's pay package?
    (A) Stock options
    (B) Bonuses
    (C) Profit sharing
    (D) Salary

3. ( ) What is a "golden parachute"?
    (A) A bonus based on a company's profits
    (B) A pay package given to all CEOs
    (C) A special contract used only by CEOs
    (D) A payment made if a firm gets a new owner

4. ( ) What was shocking about the exit package of The Home Depot's CEO?
    (A) It was huge even though the firm's stock was doing poorly.
    (B) It was paid a few months before the company went bankrupt.
    (C) It was the largest CEO exit package in corporate history.
    (D) It didn't reach the total expected by the company's workers.

5. ( ) What does the phrase *call for* in line 31 mean?
    (A) contact
    (B) demand
    (C) announce
    (D) bother

Writing about the Article   Answer each question based on the article.

1. What was the value of the exit package of Gillette's CEO?

_____

2. What do supporters of CEO pay packages say?

_____

3. What does the article say about Google and Microsoft?

_____

Vocabulary Building   Choose the best word to fill in each blank.

1. It was my _____ to redesign our name cards. We needed a fresh image.
   (A) direction   (B) decision   (C) executive   (D) performance

2. At next month's computer show, we'll have a booth. Mr. Lin will be there to
   _____ our company.
   (A) deserve   (B) contribute   (C) provide   (D) represent

3. Since the firm lost money last year, nobody received a(n) _____.
   (A) success   (B) talent   (C) bonus   (D) ownership

4. After the _____ is signed, we'll start building the new hotel.
   (A) stock   (B) debate   (C) value   (D) contract

5. When Ed got home and saw the mess the dog had made, he was _____.
   (A) furious   (B) huge   (C) comfortable   (D) average

6. I can't take _____ for closing the deal. It was Hiro's doing.
   (A) performance   (B) critic   (C) credit   (D) situation

7. After the two energy giants _____, they formed one of the world's
   largest companies.
   (A) merged   (B) deserved   (C) included   (D) attracted

8. Our CEO feels a strong sense of _____ towards the company. He wants
   us all to succeed together.
   (A) package   (B) supporter   (C) executive   (D) responsibility

Phrase Building — Write the correct phrase in each blank. (Remember to use the correct word form.)

● go through the roof ● tied to ● by and large ● hold true

Our monthly costs are _____.
Rents in our building rose 20% in June, and our electricity bills are higher than ever.
_____, there isn't much we can do about the problem. We've asked around to see how other firms are doing. They all say the same situation _____ for them. Now I'm starting to understand why so many companies are relocating to other cities. If things get much worse for us, we may need to do the same thing.

Listening Exercise Disc 2, Track 5

Listen to the conversation. Then, answer the following questions.

1. ( ) Where did the man read the news about HL Industries?
   - (A) On the Internet
   - (B) In a book
   - (C) On TV
   - (D) In a newspaper

2. ( ) When did the woman read about the company?
   - (A) Yesterday
   - (B) Last week
   - (C) A few weeks ago
   - (D) Last year

3. ( ) How much money did the company lose in 2007?
   - (A) $2 million
   - (B) $25 million
   - (C) $1 billion
   - (D) $7 billion

Listening Activity 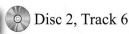 Disc 2, Track 6

Listen to the report. Then, fill in the information in the chart.

1. Where is Bluegreen based?	
2. What does the company make?	
3. How much more than the lowest-paid worker can the CEO earn?	
4. Who will receive a bonus if the company has a good year?	
5. How many people work there?	

Discussion Questions

1. What's the best way to "climb the corporate ladder"? How can a person go from entry-level worker to manager to vice president, etc.?

2. Should there be laws setting a maximum amount of money that a CEO can earn? Why or why not?

3. Along with all their power and money, CEOs are also under a lot of pressure. Would you prefer a job with high pay and high stress or low pay and low stress?

Discussion Activity

Hold a mini debate. On one side are people who think CEOs deserve high salaries. On the other side are people who think CEO salaries are too high. First, each side should spend a few minutes thinking of reasons for its point of view. Then, hold the mini debate.

Example: We think CEOs deserve their high salaries. They have to make important decisions, and that requires a lot of knowledge, experience, and hard work....

Pre-Reading Questions
Discuss these questions in pairs.

1. What big cities have you traveled to?

2. Do you live in a big city or a small town?

3. What is London famous for? (Ex: Big Ben)

Consider the Topic
Read each statement. Check if you agree or disagree with it.

	agree	disagree
1. I would like to travel to England one day.	☐	☐
2. Most big cities are too expensive!	☐	☐
3. I love visiting places that are rich in history.	☐	☐

Reading Passage Disc 2, Track 7

1   London, one of the world's great cities, has many strengths. One is its **ability**
     to grow and change with the times. Over the years, the city has faced many
     challenges, yet it has met them all, **head on**. Along the way, England's **capital**
     has developed into one of the world's most **diverse** cities. It is home to people
5   from many cultures, who add to the city's rich heritage.

     The Romans first developed the area 2,000 years ago, founding a town which
     they called Londinium. In the 11th century, the city, whose name had been
     shortened to London, became England's capital. Over the centuries, new
     leaders added their own touches. Some built great churches. Others built
10   palaces. Sites like the Tower of London, Westminster Abbey, and Buckingham
     Palace became part of the city's identity.

     However, London's history is not only one of **progress**. The city has gone
     through terrible crises. In the 14th century, 1/3 of the population died from
     a horrible disease – the Black Death. In 1666, 80% of the city burned down
15   during the Great Fire of London. And, from 1940-1941, much of the city was
     destroyed during World War II. Yet, time after time, the city has **stood tall** and
     rebuilt itself.

     London is now a leading cultural center. There are many top museums such
     as the National Gallery. The performing arts are also alive and well, with
20   frequent concerts and plays. For more **casual** entertainment, people can
     dance **to their heart's content** at night clubs. Sports lovers also have a lot to

     choose from, such as Wimbledon, a major tennis
     event. Plus, don't forget the dining scene. Six
     thousand restaurants serve food from more than
25   70 countries.

     A great way to get a feeling for this amazing city is
     by taking a ride on the London Eye. Thirty-minute
     trips carry people 500 feet into the air, offering
     excellent views. You can also see the sights on a

---

⁴ diverse – having a rich variety   ¹⁰ palace – large home (often for a king, queen, etc.)
⁵ heritage – culture/background

30   "double decker" bus. Or, to travel quickly from A to B, you can ride the Tube, London's subway system. Its 511 trains carry 6.2 million riders a day.

London's 7.3 million residents come together to form the heart and soul of the city. They include people from many cultures and regions, such as Asia, Africa, and the Caribbean. In festivals like the Notting Hill Carnival,
35   they **celebrate** their backgrounds. **Generation** after generation, every Londoner adds to the spirit of the ever-changing city.

³² heart and soul – most important part   ³³ region – area

Questions about the Reading   Choose the best answer.

1. ( ) When did the city suffer from a terrible disease?
     (A) In the 11ᵗʰ century
     (B) In the 14ᵗʰ century
     (C) In the 17ᵗʰ century
     (D) In the 20ᵗʰ century

2. ( ) What type of tragedy is NOT mentioned in the article?
     (A) A natural disaster
     (B) A major war
     (C) A horrible disease
     (D) A financial crash

3. ( ) How many places to eat does London have?
     (A) 70
     (B) 500
     (C) 511
     (D) 6,000

4. ( ) What is the Tube?
     (A) A public transportation system
     (B) A sporting event
     (C) A ride that takes people very high up
     (D) A new museum

5. ( ) Which of the following is true?
     (A) London has around 73 million residents.
     (B) The London Eye goes as high as 500 meters.
     (C) The Notting Hill Carnival is a cultural festival.
     (D) It's hard to see the city while riding a bus.

Writing about the Article
Answer each question based on the article.

1. How much of the city burned down during the Great Fire of London?

_____

2. What is one of London's top museums?

_____

3. What major tennis event is held in London every year?

_____

Vocabulary Building
Choose the best word to fill in each blank.

1. Next month, the company will _____ its 15th anniversary.
   (A) celebrate   (B) serve   (C) become   (D) found

2. To be a translator, you need to have excellent language _____.
   (A) identities   (B) challenges   (C) abilities   (D) cultures

3. It's a _____ party. Jeans will be fine.
   (A) leading   (B) casual   (C) terrible   (D) tall

4. My parents' _____ had to work hard to earn money. I think we have it easier.
   (A) history   (B) population   (C) generation   (D) entertainment

5. The house was _____ by the strong hurricane.
   (A) destroyed   (B) built   (C) offered   (D) celebrated

6. We've made a lot of _____ in repairing the roof. We should be finished soon.
   (A) strength   (B) period   (C) progress   (D) growth

7. We've got a _____ climate. On any day, it could be raining, snowing, or clear outside.
   (A) tall   (B) famous   (C) diverse   (D) cultural

8. Washington D.C. is the _____ of the USA, but it isn't the largest city.
   (A) palace   (B) capital   (C) view   (D) population

Phrase Building
Write the correct phrase in each blank. (Remember to use the correct word form.)

● head on ● along the way ● to one's heart's content ● stand tall

My brother just got his GRE test scores. He didn't score high enough to meet the requirements of the school he wants to attend. I told him to _____ and not give up. He can take the test again in a few months. Tonight, I'm taking him to his favorite restaurant, where he can eat _____. Tomorrow, he'll start preparing to take the test again. I know that if he meets the challenge _____, he'll score very high the next time around.

Listening Exercise
 Disc 2, Track 8

Listen to the conversation. Then, answer the following questions.

1. ( ) Why was the woman unable to make the booking?
   - (A) The airline does not fly to London on March 15th.
   - (B) She did not know the man's last name.
   - (C) There are no seats available that day.
   - (D) When she called British Airways, they were closed.

2. ( ) Why does the man want to fly on British Airways?
   - (A) He is a frequent flier member.
   - (B) He prefers their service.
   - (C) He gets a company discount.
   - (D) He is a citizen of the UK.

3. ( ) What does the man ask the woman to do?
   - (A) Try another airline
   - (B) Book another day
   - (C) Complain to the airline
   - (D) Cancel the reservation

Listening Activity Disc 2, Track 9

Listen to the advertisement. Then, fill in the information in the chart.

1. How many people have visited the museum?	
2. How long has the museum been open?	
3. What day is Family Day?	
4. What event will be held on Sunday afternoons in July?	
5. How many hours does that event last?	

Discussion Questions

1. Of all the London points of interest discussed in the unit's reading passage, which ones interest you the most?

2. London is a very expensive city. How about your country's capital?

3. Which of the world's great capital cities would you like to travel to?

Discussion Activity

Introduce your city to the world. Working with a few classmates, make a "mini introduction" (just a few minutes long) to your home. Some things you might talk about are its history, famous buildings, museums, places to eat, and any other interesting things you can think of.

Example: We live in Buenos Aires, one of Argentina's best cities. There's so much to see and do here. Many visitors like dancing all through the night....

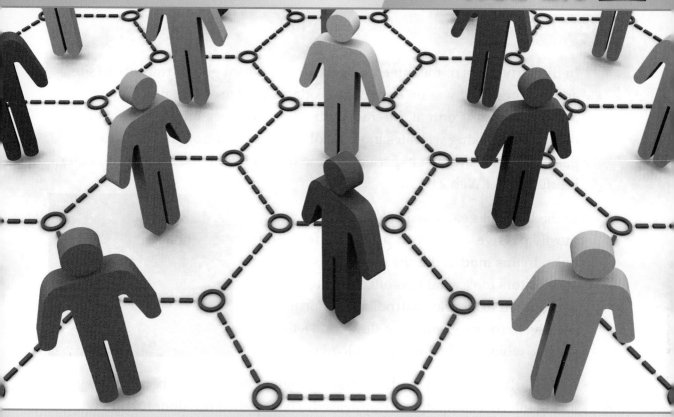

Discuss these questions in pairs.

1. What do you usually use the Internet for? (Ex: e-mail)

2. What are your favorite websites?

3. Has the Internet changed a lot in the last 5-10 years? If so, how?

Consider the Topic

Read each statement. Check if you agree or disagree with it.

	agree	disagree
1. Surfing the Internet is still too slow.	☐	☐
2. I like sharing photos on the Net.	☐	☐
3. The Net changes so quickly, it's sometimes hard to keep up!	☐	☐

Reading Passage   ◉ Disc 2, Track 10

1 In the early years of the Internet, Web surfing meant going from site to site and reading what was on each page. Today's Web users are much more **active**. They add **content**, **interact** with others, and personalize sites. Site owners are making websites more flexible, while encouraging users to

5 participate. This way of experiencing the Internet, with the user at the center, is often called Web 2.0.

In the Internet's early years, Web surfing was mostly **passive**. Users read pages and followed links. In this **model**, the site owner was **in charge**,

10 and visitors took what was offered. Interaction was limited to simple chatrooms and forums. Adding to the problem were slow connection speeds, which made it hard to upload content.

In the early 2000s, that model started changing. A huge number of money-

15 losing Internet companies **disappeared**. That **opened the door** for a new generation of interactive websites. With faster connection speeds, users could easily upload content. Users, instead of site owners, were becoming a site's most important members. The time for Web 2.0 had arrived.

The more active users become, the more democratic the Web is. Sites like

20 YouTube (for videos) and Flickr (for photos) are built with user-added content. Millions of people write their own blogs. On "wiki" sites, such as Wikipedia, members add, change, and delete information. And, on social networking sites like MySpace and Facebook, people meet and build new communities. Then there are sites like Reddit and Digg, which collect links

25 to online articles. They let users vote for their favorite articles, with the top vote-getters rising to the top. Now that's democracy in action!

As people's expectations of the Internet have changed, owners have made their sites more interactive. For example, people can change a MyYahoo page to make it look the way they want. Stores like Amazon encourage people

---

[3] personalize – make into a way you prefer
[4] flexible – changeable
[13] upload – put online (Ex: photos)
[19] democratic – giving power and choices to everyone

30   to write product **reviews**. And, news sites like CNN run polls asking for people's opinions. All these sites **go out of their way** to place the user at the center.

In some ways, Web 2.0 is not only an experience, it's a lifestyle. As the Web becomes more interactive, we don't just use it, we live in it. The Net has

35   become like a neighborhood. Around us are friends, favorite shops, and familiar places where we meet and share ideas. As we interact with others and **contribute** content, we're part of the Internet's change and growth.

---

³⁰ poll – question(s) about a topic   ³³ lifestyle – way of living

Questions about the Reading   **Choose the best answer.**

1. (   ) What is the main idea?
   - (A) Web 2.0 is another way for companies to make money online.
   - (B) Facebook is a great social networking site.
   - (C) It's fun to make changes to a MyYahoo page.
   - (D) In recent years, the Internet has become much more interactive.

2. (   ) What happened in the early 2000s?
   - (A) The first ever websites were created.
   - (B) Many online firms went out of business.
   - (C) Web connection speeds slowed down.
   - (D) Site owners tried harder to control content.

3. (   ) What is true about a "wiki"?
   - (A) People visit a wiki in order to network.
   - (B) Wikis work great as video hosting websites.
   - (C) A wiki is a blog that lets anyone add web links.
   - (D) On a wiki, the content is shaped by users.

4. (   ) How is Amazon becoming more interactive?
   - (A) By encouraging people to report news stories
   - (B) By making the site more like Yahoo
   - (C) By letting users review products
   - (D) By asking users to add links to other stores

5. (   ) What does the word *run* in line 30 mean?
   - (A) operate
   - (B) hurry
   - (C) flow
   - (D) compete

Writing about the Article — Answer each question based on the article.

1. In the early years of the Internet, why was uploading content difficult?

_____

2. What do people vote for on www.digg.com?

_____

3. How has the Web become like a neighborhood?

_____

Vocabulary Building — Choose the best word to fill in each blank.

1. The _____ on this site is excellent. Here's an article about rainforests.
   (A) center (B) democracy (C) lifestyle (D) content

2. I went into the store for a minute. When I went back out, my bike had _____!
   (A) followed (B) disappeared (C) involved (D) placed

3. Keith is one of the class's most _____ students. He asks a lot of
   questions and is happy to help his classmates.
   (A) simple (B) limited (C) active (D) familiar

4. On a camping trip, everyone has to _____. It's my job to cook the food.
   (A) contribute (B) upload (C) arrive (D) encourage

5. Selling goods below cost is an unusual business _____.
   (A) visitor (B) growth (C) model (D) link

6. While you play, you can _____ with other players using the chat box.
   (A) delete (B) involve (C) interact (D) follow

7. People at that company are very _____. They won't do anything without
   direct orders from the boss.
   (A) passive (B) favorite (C) familiar (D) important

8. Before I buy the camera, I'll read some _____ to see what other people
   think of it.
   (A) members (B) speeds (C) firms (D) reviews

Phrase Building
Write the correct phrase in each blank. (Remember to use the correct word form.)

- in charge
- get involved
- open the door
- go out of one's way

I used to be _____ of my company's human resources department. I think I was a good supervisor. When there were problems, I _____ to be fair. I listened carefully to both sides of the story before making a decision. It was a good position, but when Bob Lester retired, I asked for his old job. After all, being a division manager can _____ to bigger and better positions, like vice president. The good news is I got the job!

Listening Exercise

 Disc 2, Track 11

Listen to the conversation. Then, answer the following questions.

1. (   ) What does the man say about the Internet?
   - (A) There aren't any interesting websites.
   - (B) Some people spend too much time online.
   - (C) Web surfing is a waste of time.
   - (D) It's hard to handle so much information.

2. (   ) What site does the woman visit every day?
   - (A) Yahoo
   - (B) eBay
   - (C) Google
   - (D) CNN

3. (   ) What will the man do next?
   - (A) Visit an auction website
   - (B) Post something on his blog
   - (C) Check out a news site
   - (D) Send a link to the woman

Listening Activity Disc 2, Track 12

Listen to the report. Then, fill in the information in the chart.

1. When did the site launch?	
2. Where are the site owners from?	
3. How many photos can a member store?	
4. What's the name of the area where people chat?	
5. How may the site earn money?	

Discussion Questions

1. What kind of Net user are you? Do you post a lot (on forums and other sites) and upload a lot of content (like photos and videos)? Or, do you usually just read forums, look at photos, etc.? Or, do you do both?

2. Do some people spend too much time online? In your opinion, should people limit the amount of time they spend on the Net?

3. What would you change about the Net to improve it? Would you make it faster? Is there a type of content you'd like to see more of? What else?

Discussion Activity

There is a lot of debate about the positive and negative sides of the Internet. What's your opinion? Working in small groups of three or four classmates, come up with a list of three good points and three bad points about the Net. Then, share your list with the class.

Example: On the plus side, we think the Net is a great way to keep in touch with people. Even if you haven't seen someone for years, you can find them online....

Pre-Reading Questions — Discuss these questions in pairs.

1. Who are your favorite actors and actresses?

2. What kinds of problems do famous people have? (Ex: drinking too much)

3. Recently, have you heard any news about celebrities with big problems?

Consider the Topic — Read each statement. Check if you agree or disagree with it.

	agree	disagree
1. Celebrities have easy lives.	☐	☐
2. Movie stars and singers try too hard to look perfect.	☐	☐
3. Singers and other stars have very little privacy.	☐	☐

Reading Passage 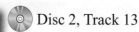 Disc 2, Track 13

1   Money. Fame. Excitement. It sounds like celebrities have the perfect life.
     Millions **look up to** them as idols. And yet, the life of a star isn't as easy as it
     looks. They face a lot of pressure on a daily basis – from studios, the media,
     and fans. We expect them to be perfect in every way. Yet, deep down, they're
5   people just like the rest of us. Sometimes, the pressure is too much to handle.
     Indeed, for every photo of a smiling superstar, there's another of a celebrity
     going through serious problems.

     For many celebrities, the trouble begins early in their careers. As soon as
     singers and actors become famous, they lose all **privacy**. Their lives become
10   public stories for the world to read about. So, stars learn to be careful about
     what they say and do. Many hire publicists – professionals who help them
     maintain a good image.

     Part of living a public life is the pressure to look **flawless**. While the rest of us
     may have wrinkles and a bit of extra weight, stars often see natural flaws as
15   career killers. So, they turn to plastic surgery to try and stay perfect. That goes
     for men and women. Sometimes, their surgeries become a big part of their
     fame. Other times, they become major gossip topics, such
     as Michael Jackson's many **operations**.

     Living under the spotlight day after day can **get to**
20   anyone. Some celebrities, unable to deal with it all, **suffer**
     from depression. A **related** problem is drug and alcohol
     abuse. A number of stars, including Marilyn Monroe and
     John Belushi, have died far too young. Some die from a
     drug overdose. Others take their own lives.

25   Some stars have spoken out about their problems and the
     issue of celebrity pressure. Brooke Shields **admitted** she
     once suffered from depression. When Owen Wilson went
     through personal problems, other actors asked the press

---

³ on a daily basis – every day
⁴ deep down – in fact/truthfully
¹⁴ wrinkles – lines in one's skin
¹⁵ plastic surgery – operation to
    change how you look

¹⁹ under the spotlight – receiving a lot of attention
²⁴ overdose – illness or death caused by taking too
    much of a drug
²⁷ depression – deep sadness

29 to leave him alone. Kate Winslet has spoken out against plastic surgery. Others, like Robert Downey Jr., have gone through tough times but have come out on top.

Perhaps over time, these voices will start to **make an impact**. For now, we still live in a world that treats stars like public **property**. For all the good news we print about them, there's just as much bad news. Learning to live
35 as a superstar is surely a lot harder than it looks.

³¹ come out on top – succeed

Questions about the Reading Choose the best answer.

1. (   ) What happens to many people after they become famous?
    (A) They begin to be careful about their actions.
    (B) They stop worrying about their image.
    (C) They start saying whatever they want.
    (D) They find they have more privacy than ever.

2. (   ) What does the article suggest about plastic surgery?
    (A) Only female movie stars want plastic surgery.
    (B) It's usually a career killer.
    (C) Stars often think it's necessary to have done.
    (D) It can't make people perfect.

3. (   ) What problem suffered by celebrities is NOT mentioned?
    (A) Drug abuse
    (B) Loneliness
    (C) Alcohol use
    (D) Depression

4. (   ) What does the article imply about celebrities?
    (A) They never speak publicly about their problems.
    (B) Many of them worry about wrinkles.
    (C) All celebrities support plastic surgery.
    (D) Once a star is in trouble, it's impossible to recover.

5. (   ) What does the word *press* in line 28 mean?
    (A) pressure
    (B) force
    (C) media
    (D) crowd

Writing about the Article
Answer each question based on the article.

1. What are some sources of the pressure faced by stars?

_____

2. What does a publicist do?

_____

3. Who are two stars that died at a young age?

_____

Vocabulary Building
Choose the best word to fill in each blank.

1. The student _____ that he cheated on the test.
   (A) spoke (B) treated (C) admitted (D) hired

2. It's private _____, so we're not allowed to park our car here.
   (A) professional (B) period (C) problem (D) property

3. Most movie-goers say the film is _____. They like everything about it.
   (A) flawless (B) recent (C) extra (D) careful

4. During the winter, many animals in the park _____ because they couldn't find enough to eat.
   (A) expected (B) maintained (C) handled (D) suffered

5. After the accident, Tom needed a(n) _____ to repair his knee.
   (A) operation (B) pressure (C) image (D) issue

6. _____ abuse can lead to serious problems. It can even cost a person his or her life.
   (A) Topic (B) Media (C) Drug (D) Fame

7. Let's go to a more quiet place to talk so we can have some _____.
   (A) privacy (B) weight (C) fame (D) voice

8. The fall in house prices is probably _____ to other problems facing the economy.
   (A) suffered (B) related (C) treated (D) printed

Phrase Building

Write the correct phrase in each blank. (Remember to use the correct word form.)

● look up to   ● get to   ● make an impact   ● go through

I've always _____ my big sister Li Pei. Not only is she smart and beautiful, but she's also a good friend. I remember when I was in high school. I stayed up until 1:00 AM almost every night, doing homework and preparing for tests. Sometimes, the pressure seriously _____ me, and I felt like I was going crazy. Li Pei was always there to encourage me. Her support really _____ on my life, and it still does. We talk on the phone at least twice a week.

Listening Exercise

 Disc 2, Track 14

Listen to the conversation. Then, answer the following questions.

1. (   ) What does the man think about child stars?
    (A) They need to work very hard.
    (B) They can't have normal childhoods.
    (C) They deal with a lot of stress.
    (D) They have a lot of advantages.

2. (   ) According to the woman, who gives child stars pressure?
    (A) Fans
    (B) Studios
    (C) Parents
    (D) Actors

3. (   ) What activity is NOT mentioned by the woman?
    (A) Playing
    (B) Traveling
    (C) Filming
    (D) Interviewing

Listening Activity 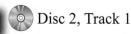 Disc 2, Track 15

Listen to the report. Then, fill in the information in the chart.

1. What is the name of the charity?	
2. Name two services it provides.	
3. How many celebrities have given money to the charity?	
4. Who owns the office building?	
5. How much money do they want to raise every year?	

Discussion Questions

1. In your opinion, what's the best and worst thing about being a superstar?

2. How do you feel about plastic surgery? Is it something you would consider having done?

3. Even when they're going through serious problems, celebrities can't hide from reporters. What's your feeling about that? Should there be laws protecting troubled stars from the media?

Discussion Activity

Make up a news report about a celebrity. First, decide which singer, actor, athlete, or other celebrity you will report on. Then, think up a problem for him or her. How long has the problem been going on? What is being done about it? Finally, prepare a short report (just a minute or two long) to share with the rest of the class.

Example: This week, Britney Spears is back in the news. Some people are saying she is over-eating again....

Pre-Reading Questions

Discuss these questions in pairs.

1. In your country, is there a big gap between the rich and poor?

2. How easy is it to go from being middle class to being rich?

3. How do you feel about the local economy? Is it in good shape? Bad shape?

Consider the Topic

Read each statement. Check if you agree or disagree with it.

	agree	disagree
1. Prices of many goods are rising very quickly.	☐	☐
2. If a person is poor now, he or she will always be poor.	☐	☐
3. The average monthly salary in this city is too low to live on.	☐	☐

Reading Passage Disc 2, Track 16

1　"The rich get richer, and the poor get poorer." It's an old saying that a lot of people feel is true. However, while many countries have a clear rich/poor divide, they also tend to have strong middle classes. But is this model **breaking down**? A popular new idea, the "M-shaped society," says that in

5　some places, it is. There is an **ongoing** debate as to whether or not Taiwan is also becoming M-shaped.

The model was **put forward** in 2006 by Japanese writer Kenichi Ohmae. He was **describing** Japan's economic changes in the 1990s. According to the model, wealth is spread out like an "M." The rich and poor are the two

10　peaks on each side of the letter. The wealthy tend to be very rich, while the poor face hard times. The middle class, in the center of the letter, is falling. As its **wages decrease**, it has a hard time improving its situation.

What about Taiwan? From the 1970s through the 1980s, Taiwan went through a so-called "economic miracle." There were jobs for everyone, and

15　daily goods were **affordable**. Recently, though, many people have noticed a big change. Prices are rising **across the board** – for food, housing, energy costs, and more. That's making a lot of people nervous.

However, according to the "M-shaped" model, wages should also be falling. Yet, that is not

20　the case in Taiwan. From 1994 to 2006, average monthly salaries in the industrial and services sectors rose from 33,689 NT to 44,107 NT. During the same **period**, salaries in the manufacturing sector also rose from 30,803 NT to 42,293 NT.

25　On the other hand, the **gap** between low and high income earners is growing. In 2006, the average yearly income for high income workers was 1.82 million NT. It was only 304,000 NT for low income workers. That's a difference of 5.99 times. In

---

³ divide – gap
³ middle class – people with average incomes
¹⁰ peak – top point

¹⁴ miracle – something incredible
²⁰ case – situation
²² sector – area/field

30 contrast, 10 years ago, the difference was 5.41 times. Also, the number of people living in poverty rose from 116,225 in 1991 to 218,151 in 2006.

So, Taiwan is clearly going through changes. The numbers show that the rich are getting richer, and there is a growing rich/poor divide. At the same time, high prices are hurting a lot of people, who say wages are

35 not rising fast enough. Time will tell if the middle class, the heart of the economy, can maintain its **strength**. Then the question of whether or not Taiwan is "M-shaped" will be easier to answer.

[36] maintain – keep

Questions about the Reading   Choose the best answer.

1. (   ) What is the main idea?
   (A) The debate continues over whether or not Taiwan is M-shaped.
   (B) In an M-shaped society, the wealthy are extremely rich.
   (C) Within a few years, most countries will be M-shaped.
   (D) The M-shaped model was based on Japan's economic situation.

2. (   ) In an M-shaped society, who faces a falling salary?
   (A) The rich
   (B) The poor
   (C) The middle class
   (D) Everybody

3. (   ) What was the last decade of Taiwan's economic miracle?
   (A) The 1970s
   (B) The 1980s
   (C) The 1990s
   (D) The 2000s

4. (   ) In 1994, what was the average monthly salary in the manufacturing sector?
   (A) 30,803 NT
   (B) 33,689 NT
   (C) 44,107 NT
   (D) 42,293 NT

5. (   ) Which of the following is true about Taiwan?
   (A) From 1994 to 2006, the average service sector salary decreased.
   (B) High income workers earned an average of 2,000,000 NT in 2006.
   (C) In 2006, the best paid workers earned 5.41 times more than low income workers.
   (D) There were more people in poverty in 2006 than in 1991.

Writing about the Article

Answer each question based on the article.

1. Who put forward the M-shaped model?

   _____

2. In Taiwan, what is happening to the prices of daily goods?

   _____

3. From 1994 to 2006, what happened to wages in Taiwan's industrial sector?

   _____

Vocabulary Building

Choose the best word to fill in each blank.

1. Queen Victoria ruled England for a long _____ of time.
   (A) center   (B) idea   (C) period   (D) income

2. The price of new computers is _____. That's good news, since I need a new one.
   (A) maintaining   (B) answering   (C) noting   (D) decreasing

3. People who work at fast food restaurants earn low _____.
   (A) wages   (B) changes   (C) models   (D) costs

4. The ring is beautiful, and it's _____. It would make a perfect gift.
   (A) nervous   (B) affordable   (C) middle   (D) low

5. Traffic in this area is still bad. It's a(n) _____ problem.
   (A) falling   (B) wealthy   (C) high   (D) ongoing

6. Look at the beautiful new houses down the street from the old and ugly ones. It shows how big the _____ between the rich and poor is.
   (A) gap   (B) service   (C) saying   (D) letter

7. How would you _____ your boss? Would you say he's easy or hard to get along with?
   (A) grow   (B) maintain   (C) describe   (D) hold

8. Theresa is very creative. It's one of her greatest _____.
   (A) situations   (B) divides   (C) questions   (D) strengths

Phrase Building

Write the correct phrase in each blank. (Remember to use the correct word form.)

● break down   ● according to   ● put forward   ● across the board

In the past, people felt safe at their jobs. They believed that if they worked hard, their company would take care of them. With the economy in bad shape, that system is starting to _____. The unemployment rate is rising, making everyone nervous. _____, positions from manager to delivery person are being cut. In some companies, workers are _____ interesting ideas to save their jobs. At some firms, employees are even offering to take pay cuts if the boss will agree not to fire anyone.

Listening Exercise   Disc 2, Track 17

Listen to the conversation. Then, answer the following questions.

1. (   ) What kind of job is the woman looking for?
   (A) Fashion designer
   (B) Package designer
   (C) Furniture designer
   (D) Interior designer

2. (   ) Why doesn't the woman want to apply for the job?
   (A) The salary isn't high enough.
   (B) The firm is far from her house.
   (C) The company isn't famous.
   (D) The work is too difficult.

3. (   ) What does she pay a lot for every month?
   (A) Food
   (B) Clothes
   (C) Rent
   (D) Entertainment

Listening Activity Disc 2, Track 18

Listen to the report. Then, fill in the information in the chart.

1. Name two basic items that are becoming more expensive.	
2. How much may food prices rise?	
3. How much may home energy costs rise?	
4. Name two office supplies with rising prices.	
5. What is the main cause of higher prices?	

Discussion Questions

1. In your daily life, which goods are becoming more expensive?

2. In some countries, rich people pay very high taxes. Poor and middle class workers pay low taxes. Is that fair? Why or why not?

3. What's your sense of the future? Do you think the economy will get better or worse? Why?

Discussion Activity

Some people say the youth of today have easier lives than their parents did. Others say the young generation faces a new set of problems. Hold a mini debate. On one side are 2-3 classmates holding the first point of view. On the other side are 2-3 classmates with the opposite viewpoint. First, spend a few minutes thinking of reasons for your position. Then, hold the mini debate.

Example: Young people work a lot less than people from their parents' generation. These days, most people have a two-day weekend, which few people had 30 years ago....

Pre-Reading Questions
Discuss these questions in pairs.

1. Would you like to travel into space? If so, where to?

2. Would you like to live on another planet? Why or why not?

3. Look at the picture. What do you think is happening?

Consider the Topic
Read each statement. Check if you agree or disagree with it.

	agree	disagree
1. There is life on other planets.	☐	☐
2. Projects like the International Space Station cost too much money.	☐	☐
3. One day, people will live on the moon.	☐	☐

Reading Passage Disc 2, Track 19

1   For many years, there have been books, movies, and TV shows about outer
    space. People have long **wondered** if there's life on other planets. At the same
    time, writers have wondered if people might live on the moon or elsewhere
    some day.

5   We've already made several short trips to the moon. As part of the USA's
    Apollo space program, six landings were made from 1969 to 1972. The longest
    stays on the moon lasted about three days each. Astronauts set up **temporary**
    bases and ran **experiments**. On the last three visits, they brought an LRV
    (Lunar Rover Vehicle), a car that ran on batteries. They were able to drive
10 many kilometers around the landing areas.

    Most trips into space, however, **tend to** be much closer
    to Earth. Since 2000, people have been living on the
    International Space Station, a joint project of the USA,
    European Space Agency, Japan, Canada, and Russia.
15 We've also gone on many "space walks" to install
    equipment, make repairs, and carry out experiments.

    Now that we know a lot about living in space, where
    should we build colonies? Because of their closeness to
    Earth, the moon and Mars are the most likely locations.
20 In fact, NASA, the USA's space agency, has a long-term
    plan to set up a colony on Mars. Also, China's space
    agency plans to send people to the moon, with a long-
    term goal of setting up a colony there.

    However, we still face many challenges before a space colony will be possible.
25 First, we need to come up with a cheaper way to **transport** the necessary
    equipment. Also, we need to find **locations** for colonies near a water **source**.
    A good deal of water will be needed for drinking, washing, and other uses.
    Furthermore, we need to find a way to produce fuel on the colony, for
    cooking, heating, and trips back to Earth.

---

7 astronaut – person who travels in space   22 long-term – over a long period of time
13 joint project – job done together   28 fuel – energy source
18 colony – new area where people live

30 Despite these challenges, many people believe it is our destiny to travel and
live in space. Others think there are more important problems that must
be addressed on Earth, such as hunger and disease. The most **optimistic**
people feel that technology and medicine will continue to improve. That
will let us meet all these challenges at the same time. Indeed, within 50
35 years, a number of us may be living on another planet, looking back at
Earth from a very different **point of view**.

30 destiny – something that is meant to be; fate   32 addressed – handled

Questions about the Reading   Choose the best answer.

1. (   ) What is the main idea?
   (A) Since space travel is expensive, many people disagree with it.
   (B) Though it won't be easy, people may soon live on other planets.
   (C) The International Space Station is our greatest achievement.
   (D) Above all, people need water to survive.

2. (   ) What does the article suggest about the Apollo moon landings?
   (A) They did not include long stays on the moon by people.
   (B) They were among many trips taken by people into deep space.
   (C) They were made to set up a long-term colony there.
   (D) They took place after the International Space Station was built.

3. (   ) Why is Mars a good choice for a space colony?
   (A) The planet has very good weather.
   (B) People have already made trips there.
   (C) Mars is very close to the sun.
   (D) It is not too far from our planet.

4. (   ) Which of the following is NOT a challenge involved with space colonies?
   (A) Learning how to perform a space walk
   (B) Finding a way to heat our homes
   (C) Inventing new means of transportation
   (D) Locating a spot near a water source

5. (   ) Why are some people against further space travel?
   (A) They don't believe space can teach us anything.
   (B) They want us to address other problems first.
   (C) They think the technology being used is unsafe.
   (D) They worry the colonies won't be able to last long.

Writing about the Article

Answer each question based on the article.

1. What do people do during space walks?

   _____

2. What plan does NASA have for Mars?

   _____

3. Why does a space colony need to be near water?

   _____

Vocabulary Building

Choose the best word to fill in each blank.

1. The park would be a good _____ for the party. There are tables and chairs, and we could play baseball.
   (A) planet   (B) project   (C) location   (D) goal

2. After the goods leave the factory, a ship _____ them overseas.
   (A) installs   (B) builds   (C) produces   (D) transports

3. Things look bad now, but I am _____ that they will get better.
   (A) possible   (B) optimistic   (C) different   (D) cheap

4. The job will be very expensive. _____, it will take a long time to complete.
   (A) Since   (B) Despite   (C) However   (D) Furthermore

5. I _____ what it would be like to study in another country.
   (A) believe   (B) travel   (C) wonder   (D) live

6. We've developed a new kind of fuel. Next month, we'll run our first _____ to see how well it works.
   (A) experiment (B) agency   (C) disease   (D) planet

7. They've found the _____ of the problem. One of the wires was loose.
   (A) trip   (B) source   (C) plan   (D) space

8. This is just a(n) _____ sign. We'll put up a better one soon.
   (A) temporary   (B) important   (C) short   (D) close

Phrase Building Write the correct phrase in each blank.

● tend to   ● a good deal of   ● at the same time   ● point of view

One of my household chores is cleaning the garage. I don't mind so much, since it's where I build my robots. That's an old hobby of mine. Anyway, according to my parents' _____, I should always be the one to clean the garage, since I use it more than anyone. I guess that makes sense, since it does _____ get messy when I work there. The good news is the garage is huge. So, after designing a robot, I have _____ space to build it!

Listening Exercise   Disc 2, Track 20

Listen to the conversation. Then, answer the following questions.

1. (   ) What are the people talking about?
   (A) A project to build a space station
   (B) A budget cut for the space agency
   (C) A planned colony on another planet
   (D) A movie they saw about space travel

2. (   ) How does the man feel about the space agency's news?
   (A) He doesn't agree with it.
   (B) He thinks it's funny.
   (C) He doubts it's true.
   (D) He is surprised by it.

3. (   ) How much longer may it take to complete the project?
   (A) 5 years
   (B) 10 years
   (C) 20 years
   (D) 30 years

Listening Activity Disc 2, Track 21

Listen to the report. Then, fill in the information in the chart.

1. Where is the scientist from?	
2. What is the name of the magazine?	
3. How much cheaper may trips be in 2020?	
4. What supplies will become easier to produce?	
5. Where will important experiments be performed?	

Discussion Questions

1. How do TV shows and movies usually show life in outer space?

2. Do you think people will be living on space colonies 50 years from now? Why or why not?

3. Should we work hard to improve space travel, or should we focus on our problems on Earth? (Or, can we do both?)

Discussion Activity

Imagine you and a few classmates have been chosen to build a space colony. However, the ship that will take you there has very limited room. What are the 10 most important things you will need to bring? Make a list and compare it to those of other groups.

Example: #1: An MP3 player. We can't imagine living without our music!

#2: Our dogs and cats. We wouldn't want to leave them behind on Earth.

Pre-Reading Questions

Discuss these questions in pairs.

1. What do office workers gossip about?

2. What problems can be caused by gossip?

3. Is it all right to gossip a little, or does gossip always cause trouble?

Consider the Topic

Read each statement. Check if you agree or disagree with it.

	agree	disagree
1. It's fun to gossip about friends and colleagues.	☐	☐
2. Gossip is a good way for information to spread within a company.	☐	☐
3. I stay away from people who gossip too much.	☐	☐

Reading Passage Disc 2, Track 22

1   In today's offices, gossip is as common as ever. **Rumors**, half-truths, and
lies fly from desk to desk and employee to employee. Thanks to modern
technology, gossip can spread through an entire company within seconds.
Though it's hard to stop completely, it needs to be **kept in check**. **Otherwise**,
5   it can cause trouble for one's colleagues or even harm the company.

Office workers tend to gossip about two main areas. The first is a company's
general goings-on – hiring and firing news, yearly bonuses, and so on. As
one US survey showed, almost two-thirds of office workers **participate** in
this type of gossip. Some experts believe that, in small doses, that's actually
10   a good thing. As company news spreads, it gives employees a sense of what
management is planning. And, when managers hear something **on the
grapevine**, it helps them understand the company's morale level.

The second type of gossip **concerns** other employees. Some people love to
talk about their colleagues' romantic interests, career goals, and private lives.
15   Again, some analysts suggest that a small amount of personal gossip helps
build group **relationships**. It shows that people care about their colleagues.
However, when spread with bad intentions, it can hurt people's feelings, job
performance, and even their health.

Gossip is often **passed around** in employee break rooms
20   and around desks. Instant messaging (IM) programs are
also major gossip channels. A recent survey in England
showed that some 20% of employees use IM programs
to talk about each other. E-mail is another widely used
method. However, as many companies keep records
25   of e-mails and IM conversations, employees need to be
careful about what they type.

Most people strongly dislike being gossiped about. In a
2007 US survey, 60% of office workers viewed gossip as
the biggest office-related problem. Victims of gossip may

---

[7] goings-on – happenings/activities   [12] morale – general feeling/attitude
[8] survey – poll about a topic   [15] analyst – person who studies a topic
[9] doses – amounts   [17] intention – purpose/reason

30   even sue a company for not doing enough to stop the problem. As a result, some companies have policies that limit or **forbid** office gossip.

In general, experts say it's all right to listen to gossip as it moves along the grapevine. That way, you'll know what's happening in the company. However, one should be careful not to spread too much gossip oneself,

35   since it can lead to trouble. Nobody wants a reputation as the company's main gossiper. Not only will it cause others to lose trust in you, but it could even cost you your job.

³⁰ sue – file a legal charge against a person, company, etc.   ³¹ policy – rule

Questions about the Reading Choose the best answer.

1. (   ) According to the article, why may gossip be good for a company?
    (A) It gives employees something to talk about.
    (B) It's a way for people to learn about a company's plans.
    (C) It makes an office a lot more interesting.
    (D) It's something everybody does, but nobody admits to.

2. (   ) What topic of office gossip is NOT mentioned in the article?
    (A) Yearly pay bonuses
    (B) Recently fired people
    (C) Colleagues' monthly salaries
    (D) Employees' private lives

3. (   ) What percentage of US office workers thinks gossip is a serious problem?
    (A) 20%
    (B) 33%
    (C) 60%
    (D) 66%

4. (   ) Why do people need to be careful about using computers to gossip?
    (A) The company might keep a record of what you say.
    (B) The gossip may be printed out by another colleague.
    (C) The other person could post the gossip on a blog.
    (D) The information will spread too quickly that way.

5. (   ) What does the phrase *cost you your job* in line 37 mean?
    (A) cause your gossip to be spread
    (B) force you to pay money
    (C) lead to your being fired
    (D) offer you another position

Writing about the Article
Answer each question based on the article.

1. What can happen when gossip is spread with bad intentions?

_____

2. What may a victim of office gossip do?

_____

3. What do experts say office workers should be careful not to do?

_____

Vocabulary Building
Choose the best word to fill in each blank.

1. If you want to _____ in the event, you have to send this form in today.
   (A) happen   (B) participate   (C) spread   (D) suggest

2. Don't believe that _____ about people getting fired. It isn't true.
   (A) rumor   (B) career   (C) area   (D) bonus

3. The _____ feeling among employees is positive. Only a few people are worried about the future.
   (A) general   (B) useful   (C) careful   (D) modern

4. My boss and I have an excellent _____. We get along very well.
   (A) colleague   (B) management   (C) channel   (D) relationship

5. Next week, the company will carry out its yearly _____ reviews. Employees with the highest scores will receive a pay bonus.
   (A) gossip   (B) speed   (C) technology   (D) performance

6. I can take everybody to the party in my car. _____, we can take a taxi.
   (A) Almost   (B) However   (C) Otherwise   (D) When

7. Don't _____ yourself with the problems caused by Phil. There's nothing you can do about them.
   (A) cause   (B) fire   (C) believe   (D) concern

8. Most parents _____ young children from staying up past midnight.
   (A) improve   (B) forbid   (C) suggest   (D) cause

Phrase Building
Write the correct phrase in each blank. (Remember to use the correct word form.)

● keep something in check   ● tend to   ● on the grapevine   ● pass around

The mood is very bad at Zephyr, Inc. As profits fall and morale sinks, employees are worried they will lose their jobs. During breaks, they get together to share rumors that they've heard _____. There's even a list of "at risk" departments being _____. The situation is bad, but management doesn't know how to _____. As a result, employees are becoming more and more nervous. To prepare for the worst, some have started looking for jobs elsewhere.

Listening Exercise   Disc 2, Track 23

Listen to the conversation. Then, answer the following questions.

1. (   ) Who are they talking about?
   (A) An important client
   (B) A new employee
   (C) A former supervisor
   (D) A vice president

2. (   ) What happened to Richard?
   (A) He was promoted.
   (B) He retired.
   (C) He switched companies.
   (D) He was fired.

3. (   ) What is the man planning to do?
   (A) Quit his job
   (B) Study the job market
   (C) Contact Richard
   (D) Hire the woman

Listening Activity Disc 2, Track 24

Listen to the announcement. Then, fill in the information in the chart.

1. What kind of company is it?	
2. What are people worried about?	
3. What must stop immediately?	
4. What is the merger important for?	
5. Who can answer people's questions?	

Discussion Questions

1. Have you ever been the victim of untrue rumors being spread about you? What happened?

2. If you were the owner of a company, would you ban employees from gossiping? Why or why not?

3. Do you agree that a small amount of gossip in a company is a good thing? Why or why not?

Discussion Activity

Play the "grapevine" game. First, one classmate should write down a piece of gossip about a colleague. (If you don't have a job, that doesn't matter. Just make one up!) Then, tell the gossip to just ONE classmate. (Nobody else should hear it.) That classmate should then tell the gossip to another classmate, and so on. The final classmate on the grapevine should repeat the gossip to the entire class. Compare it to the original gossip to see how similar or different it is!

Example: Mr. Lee is vice president of customer relations. Well, I heard that he actually yelled at a customer last week....

Pre-Reading Questions

Discuss these questions in pairs.

1. Do you do any kinds of art yourself? If so, what kinds?

2. In your country, what are some traditional handicrafts?

3. What are some products that used to be made by hand, but which are now made in factories? (Ex: furniture)

Consider the Topic

Read each statement. Check if you agree or disagree with it.

	agree	disagree
1. I prefer factory-made over handmade goods.	☐	☐
2. I like to attend arts and crafts shows.	☐	☐
3. The government should encourage people to continue making traditional crafts.	☐	☐

Reading Passage Disc 2, Track 25

1   In the past, nearly everything was made by hand. Craftspeople made cups, chairs, and other items that were both useful and beautiful. However, over time, machines and **factories** became the main producers of goods. That has led to the disappearance of some handicrafts. Fortunately, many others have
5   been kept **alive** through public interest in arts and crafts.

One lost art is the illuminated manuscript. Like all books in Europe up until 1450, they were made by hand. In an illuminated manuscript, the words were first copied onto a page. Then, beautiful borders and illustrations were added. The first letter of
10 a chapter was often made **especially** large and colorful. Paints made from natural **materials** provided the color. Using thin strips of gold (called gold leaf) could really bring a design to life. However, making these **treasures** was expensive
15 and **time-consuming**. So, after the printing press was invented, fewer and fewer were made.

A more recent art form replaced by new technology is the hand-painted theater poster. In the mid-late 20th century, going to the movies in Taiwan had a special touch. Outside theaters, one could see large paintings advertising the
20 newest films. To make one, an artist started with a small movie poster. From that, a much larger version was painted. It **emphasized** the main actors and actresses, whose names were painted in large letters. After just a few decades, this art form was replaced by large posters made with modern printing methods.

25 The good news is people in many countries are interested in handicrafts. They learn skills by reading books and magazines, or by attending classes. This has helped **preserve** many arts such as pottery and jewelry making. At shows, craftspeople sell their goods and chat with shoppers, just as they did 1,000 years ago. Governments are also helping. For example, the Crafts Council of

---

3 producers – makers
4 handicrafts – items made by hand
6 illuminated – brightly/colorfully made
6 manuscript – book

9 illustrations – pictures
12 strips – long pieces
15 printing press – machine that prints pages
21 version – type/kind

30   India helps craftspeople find new selling opportunities. Many of them meet up once a year at the Kamala show to share ideas and sell their goods.

Modern technology has influenced our lives in many positive ways. Yet, people still **appreciate** the personal touch of a handmade good. Making and buying traditional crafts are also ways to celebrate one's culture.

35   Unfortunately, not all lost arts can be brought back. But even when they **die out**, museums give us a chance to appreciate the care and effort that **went into** them.

Questions about the Reading   Choose the best answer.

1. (   ) What is suggested about the goods made by craftspeople?
   (A) They have a practical use.
   (B) They are usually very expensive.
   (C) They have all disappeared.
   (D) They look like factory-made items.

2. (   ) What does the article say about illuminated manuscripts?
   (A) Borders were added before the words were copied to a page.
   (B) Thick pieces of gold leaf were often used in them.
   (C) It took a lot of time and money to make one.
   (D) They were made popular by the invention of the printing press.

3. (   ) What was painted in large letters on hand-painted movie posters?
   (A) The names of the actors and actresses
   (B) The name of the movie theater
   (C) The name of the poster artist
   (D) The name of the movie studio

4. (   ) What part of the world hosts the Kamala show?
   (A) East Asia
   (B) South Asia
   (C) Europe
   (D) North America

5. (   ) Which of the following is true?
   (A) In Taiwan, handmade theater posters are still widely seen.
   (B) The Kamala show is held once a month.
   (C) Museums rarely display traditional crafts.
   (D) Inks used for illuminated manuscripts were all-natural.

Writing about the Article
Answer each question based on the article.

1. In illuminated manuscripts, what was special about a chapter's first letter?

_____

2. When making movie posters, what did Taiwanese artists start with?

_____

3. These days, what are some ways people learn to make handicrafts?

_____

Vocabulary Building
Choose the best word to fill in each blank.

1. Shoes, belts, and wallets can all be made at this _____.
   (A) influence   (B) factory   (C) culture   (D) theater

2. We _____ all your help. Is there anything we can do for you in return?
   (A) invent   (B) advertise   (C) copy   (D) appreciate

3. Five days after disappearing in the mountains, the hiker was found hurt, but _____.
   (A) alive   (B) special   (C) modern   (D) personal

4. The airplane pilot _____ the importance of wearing seatbelts during takeoff and landing.
   (A) attended   (B) emphasized   (C) interested   (D) became

5. The jewels are one of our country's greatest _____.
   (A) paintings   (B) treasures   (C) classes   (D) museums

6. It's a(n) _____ big case. We can't make any mistakes.
   (A) fortunately   (B) greatly   (C) nearly   (D) especially

7. Holidays and festivals help a country _____ its culture.
   (A) provide   (B) replace   (C) preserve   (D) create

8. What _____ is the shirt made of? Is it cotton?
   (A) material   (B) form   (C) version   (D) skill

Phrase Building

Write the correct phrase in each blank. (Remember to use the correct word form.)

● time-consuming   ● meet up   ● die out   ● go into

A lot of work _____ making one of these necklaces. The beads, shells, and other materials are carefully chosen one by one. Also, no two necklaces are exactly alike, so each one is special. Creating one is a _____ process, taking many hours per piece. We love what we do, but some of us are worried. We're concerned that our craft will _____ unless we get more young people involved. So, starting next year, we will offer classes to teach people the craft.

Listening Exercise

 Disc 2, Track 26

Listen to the conversation. Then, answer the following questions.

1. (   ) What does the man plan to do?
     (A) Fly somewhere to see a relative
     (B) Make time to attend the art fair
     (C) Keep the woman company
     (D) Spend time with his brother

2. (   ) Where is Jack Winters from?
     (A) Vancouver
     (B) Winnipeg
     (C) Toronto
     (D) Montreal

3. (   ) What does Mr. Winters make?
     (A) Tools
     (B) Metal doors
     (C) Knives
     (D) Pottery

Listening Activity Disc 2, Track 27

Listen to the report. Then, fill in the information in the chart.

1. What does a quilt cover?	
2. When did many American families make their own quilts?	
3. What goes inside a quilt?	
4. When did interest in quilts grow again?	
5. Who enjoys making quilts together?	

Discussion Questions

1. How do you feel about so many traditional crafts being replaced by factory-made goods? Is that a good thing? Bad thing? Neither?

2. In your country, if a person is interested in a craft (such as bead work), how can he or she learn the skills to practice it?

3. In many countries, there is a new interest in arts and crafts. People sell handmade goods (like jewelry) at shows, flea markets, etc. How about in your country?

Discussion Activity

The government has given you $30,000 to promote traditional arts. Work in groups of three or four classmates. First, think of which arts you would like to promote. Next, decide how you will spend the money. For example, will you hold a show? Will you set up classes? After you decide on a plan, tell it to the rest of the class.

Example: We want to promote handmade sweaters, which used to be common. Our plan is to hold a contest....

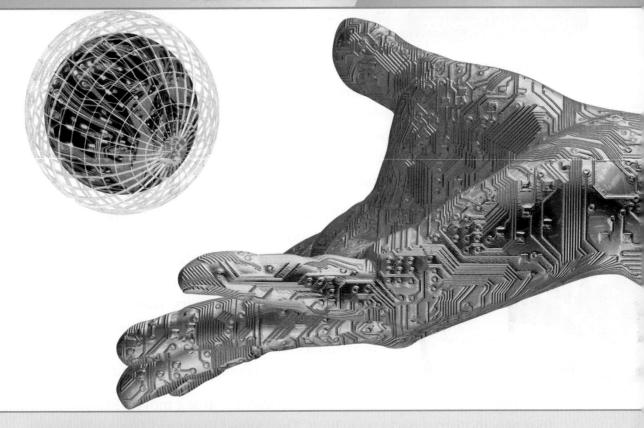

Pre-Reading Questions
Discuss these questions in pairs.

1. What are some of the biggest companies in your country?

2. Have you ever attended a computer or electronics show? Where?

3. Which hi-tech fields will be important in 20 years?

Consider the Topic
Read each statement. Check if you agree or disagree with it.

	agree	disagree
1. I'm interested in working in a hi-tech field.	☐	☐
2. The government should spend more to support hi-tech businesses.	☐	☐
3. Hi-tech industries are very important for the future of the country.	☐	☐

Reading Passage Disc 2, Track 28

1 In the global economy, countries have to keep pushing forward to stay ahead of the **competition**. That means being part of today's hottest fields while investing in next-generation industries. Thanks to its focus on the **hi-tech sector**, Taiwan is **well-positioned** to **remain** one of the world's top economies.

5 From Taipei to Kaohsiung, Taiwan's businesses, universities, and **research** centers are inventing the future together.

In 2007, Taiwan was ranked as the world's 20th largest economy. That's a great **achievement**, as the population is smaller than that of many other top
10 countries. A key reason for this success is Taiwan's hi-tech sector. For many years, Taiwan has led the world's semiconductor industry. It's also one of the top producers of LCD screens. The list goes on, from cell phones to notebook computers and more.

15 Focused on the future, Taiwan continues making strong moves. Recently, four new industrial parks were built. They joined the world-famous Hsinchu Industrial Park as hi-tech centers. In the north, the Nankang park focuses on software. Central Taiwan's park supports six fields, including bio-tech (ex: bio-batteries) and photo electronics (ex: LCDs). One of the two new parks
20 in southern Taiwan is a research and development center. The other is huge, with 50,000 workers. By 2007, it had brought in revenues of 331.3 billion NT.

An important part of this hi-tech movement is nanotechnology. It's the science of **manufacturing** large or small products very **precisely**. Some of Taiwan's biggest companies, including Taiwan Semiconductor, Formosa Plastic, and
25 Tong Yuan, are using this modern production method. And, more than 70 Taiwanese universities have **taken part in** nanotechnology research projects.

Taiwan's government has spent billions of NT supporting the hi-tech sector. It also has a three-stage plan to make it bigger and better. The first stage is using modern methods to make products like plastics and fibers. The second stage is

---

^{12} semiconductor - a basic part of many electronic products ^{21} revenues – earnings
^{16} industrial park – place with many offices and factories ^{29} fibers – threads (Ex: cotton)

30 the spread of Information Communication Technology (ICT) in areas like computer memory and semiconductors. The third stage is the development of the energy and bio-tech fields.

With all these advantages, it's no wonder so many foreign companies are investing in Taiwan. Besides its factories and research centers, Taiwan has

35 another secret weapon – its people. The Taiwanese are among the highest educated in the world. Indeed, this excellent workforce will **form the backbone of** Taiwan's hi-tech future.

[35] secret weapon – powerful advantage   [36] workforce – working people

Questions about the Reading   Choose the best answer.

1. (   ) What is suggested about Taiwan's economy?
   (A) In 2007, the economy was the world's 30th largest.
   (B) LCD screens are Taiwan's biggest exports.
   (C) The size of the population is key to Taiwan's economic growth.
   (D) Hi-tech industries are an important part of its success.

2. (   ) What part of Taiwan has an industrial park focusing on software?
   (A) Eastern Taiwan
   (B) Central Taiwan
   (C) Southern Taiwan
   (D) Northern Taiwan

3. (   ) How many schools have been involved in nanotechnology research?
   (A) Exactly 3
   (B) Less than 50
   (C) More than 70
   (D) About 331

4. (   ) What is true about the government's plan for the hi-tech sector?
   (A) There are a total of four stages in the plan.
   (B) The spread of ICT will be important in the second stage.
   (C) A total of one billion NT will be spent.
   (D) Plastics and fibers will be the third stage's main products.

5. (   ) What does the word *moves* in line 15 mean?
   (A) actions
   (B) exchanges
   (C) transfers
   (D) transports

117

Writing about the Article
Answer each question based on the article.

1. What are some Taiwanese companies that use nanotechnology?

_____

2. What are two fields supported by the industrial park in central Taiwan?

_____

3. What does the article say about the general education level in Taiwan?

_____

Vocabulary Building
Choose the best word to fill in each blank.

1. Even though it's 30 years old, it _____ my favorite movie.
   (A) remains   (B) invests   (C) continues   (D) focuses

2. The report was very _____ written. It included a huge number of details.
   (A) partly   (B) secretly   (C) precisely   (D) differently

3. Winning the award was a great _____ for the young singer.
   (A) product   (B) workforce   (C) field   (D) achievement

4. Most people enjoy using _____ products like cell phones, but few understand how they're made.
   (A) method   (B) success   (C) hi-tech   (D) memory

5. _____ continues into ways to make the batteries last longer.
   (A) Research   (B) Movement   (C) Software   (D) Industry

6. Now that the store across the street has closed, we have very little _____.
   (A) population   (B) economy   (C) science   (D) competition

7. The raw materials _____ makes up 20% of their economy.
   (A) advantage   (B) university   (C) sector   (D) support

8. It takes a lot of water and other resources to _____ the product.
   (A) manufacture   (B) rank   (C) invest   (D) succeed

Phrase Building — Write the correct phrase in each blank.

● on and on   ● well-positioned   ● form the backbone of   ● take part in

For 10 years, our software firm has been growing locally. Our president thinks we're _____ to grow into a regional leader. So, when we heard a new industrial park was opening nearby, we applied to join. We plan to open a new research and development center there. Business software will probably _____ the first group of projects. As the head engineer, I'll _____ a lot of meetings over the coming months. We have some big decisions to make!

Listening Exercise   Disc 2, Track 29

Listen to the conversation. Then, answer the following questions.

1. (   ) What will the people do in a few weeks?
   (A) Go on a trip together
   (B) Start a training program
   (C) Graduate from school
   (D) Take several more classes

2. (   ) What kind of work will the man probably do?
   (A) Design hardware
   (B) Research computers
   (C) Sell electronics
   (D) Write software

3. (   ) Why does the woman want to work in a lab?
   (A) It's peaceful.
   (B) It sounds fun.
   (C) It pays well.
   (D) It's very easy.

Listening Activity Disc 2, Track 30

Listen to the report. Then, fill in the information in the chart.

1. Where did they talk to people?	
2. What percentage uses a computer daily?	
3. What percentage said computers are important for their schoolwork?	
4. Name one popular use of computers for schoolwork.	
5. What happened to one person's phone?	

Discussion Questions

1. How can parents and schools help young people grow up with more hi-tech skills and knowledge?

2. Besides setting up industrial parks, what else can the government do to support the hi-tech sector?

3. As technology is always changing, so are the skills needed for hi-tech jobs. How can someone in a hi-tech field keep up with all the changes?

Discussion Activity

How do you see the future? Working with a few classmates, make a list of three ways that life will be very different in 100 years. You might consider work, medicine, or anything else about daily life. Use your imagination! After you're finished, read your list to the rest of the class.

Example: First, we don't think anyone will drive to work. There will be subway lines on every street, so people will board a subway train right outside their house....

Target Word List

☐ ability	Unit 13		☐ create	Unit 5
☐ achievement	Unit 20		☐ credit	Unit 12
☐ active	Unit 14		☐ critic	Unit 9
☐ admit	Unit 15		☐ data	Unit 9
☐ advise	Unit 11		☐ decision	Unit 12
☐ affordable	Unit 16		☐ decrease	Unit 16
☐ alive	Unit 19		☐ describe	Unit 16
☐ amateur	Unit 7		☐ destroy	Unit 13
☐ appear	Unit 2		☐ disappear	Unit 14
☐ appreciate	Unit 19		☐ distance	Unit 6
☐ bonus	Unit 12		☐ diverse	Unit 13
☐ breakthrough	Unit 1		☐ dominate	Unit 7
☐ capital	Unit 13		☐ drawback	Unit 4
☐ casual	Unit 13		☐ drug	Unit 15
☐ celebrate	Unit 13		☐ efficient	Unit 10
☐ chemical	Unit 3		☐ effort	Unit 3
☐ combination	Unit 2		☐ elderly	Unit 11
☐ comfortable	Unit 5		☐ emphasize	Unit 19
☐ comment	Unit 5		☐ especially	Unit 19
☐ competition	Unit 20		☐ estimate	Unit 9
☐ concern	Unit 18		☐ experiment	Unit 17
☐ confidence	Unit 7		☐ explore	Unit 8
☐ consequence	Unit 10		☐ extensive	Unit 8
☐ consistent	Unit 6		☐ factory	Unit 19
☐ content	Unit 14		☐ familiar	Unit 10
☐ contract	Unit 12		☐ feature	Unit 5
☐ contribute	Unit 14		☐ flawless	Unit 15
☐ controversy	Unit 1		☐ flow	Unit 7
☐ convert	Unit 11		☐ forbid	Unit 18

☐ franchise	Unit 4	☐ monster	Unit 5
☐ frequently	Unit 3	☐ nature	Unit 8
☐ furious	Unit 12	☐ nevertheless	Unit 4
☐ furthermore	Unit 17	☐ obvious	Unit 6
☐ gap	Unit 16	☐ ongoing	Unit 16
☐ gather	Unit 9	☐ operation	Unit 15
☐ general	Unit 18	☐ opportunity	Unit 2
☐ generation	Unit 13	☐ opposite	Unit 3
☐ hi-tech	Unit 20	☐ optimistic	Unit 17
☐ impact	Unit 7	☐ organ	Unit 1
☐ independence	Unit 4	☐ original	Unit 5
☐ informative	Unit 2	☐ otherwise	Unit 18
☐ install	Unit 10	☐ participate	Unit 18
☐ intensively	Unit 11	☐ passive	Unit 14
☐ interact	Unit 14	☐ patient	Unit 1
☐ invade	Unit 6	☐ perform	Unit 7
☐ laboratory	Unit 1	☐ performance	Unit 18
☐ license	Unit 4	☐ period	Unit 16
☐ lifestyle	Unit 10	☐ potential	Unit 1
☐ location	Unit 17	☐ precisely	Unit 20
☐ maintain	Unit 2	☐ preserve	Unit 19
☐ manufacture	Unit 20	☐ previous	Unit 3
☐ marketing	Unit 4	☐ privacy	Unit 15
☐ massive	Unit 2	☐ produce	Unit 10
☐ material	Unit 19	☐ progress	Unit 13
☐ measure	Unit 2	☐ project	Unit 10
☐ merge	Unit 12	☐ pronunciation	Unit 6
☐ minimum	Unit 8	☐ proper	Unit 8
☐ model	Unit 14	☐ property	Unit 15

☐ purchase	Unit 9		☐ taste	Unit 3
☐ pursuit	Unit 7		☐ temporary	Unit 17
☐ related	Unit 15		☐ terrific	Unit 7
☐ relationship	Unit 18		☐ toxic	Unit 11
☐ release	Unit 10		☐ track	Unit 9
☐ remain	Unit 20		☐ train	Unit 8
☐ remarkable	Unit 11		☐ transport	Unit 17
☐ repair	Unit 8		☐ treasure	Unit 19
☐ represent	Unit 12		☐ trust	Unit 4
☐ reproduce	Unit 1		☐ typically	Unit 8
☐ research	Unit 20		☐ vast	Unit 11
☐ resource	Unit 2		☐ version	Unit 6
☐ responsibility	Unit 12		☐ vitamin	Unit 3
☐ restore	Unit 11		☐ wage	Unit 16
☐ restriction	Unit 1		☐ wonder	Unit 17
☐ review	Unit 14			
☐ reward	Unit 4			
☐ risk	Unit 9			
☐ rumor	Unit 18			
☐ season	Unit 3			
☐ sector	Unit 20			
☐ security	Unit 9			
☐ separate	Unit 6			
☐ source	Unit 17			
☐ specialty	Unit 5			
☐ standard	Unit 6			
☐ strange	Unit 5			
☐ strength	Unit 16			
☐ suffer	Unit 15			

Target Phrase List

☐ a good deal of	Unit 17	☐ look up to	Unit 15
☐ across the board	Unit 16	☐ make an impact	Unit 15
☐ bit by bit	Unit 9	☐ nothing new	Unit 11
☐ break down	Unit 16	☐ odds are	Unit 7
☐ by and large	Unit 12	☐ on a regular basis	Unit 2
☐ catch the eye of	Unit 2	☐ on the grapevine	Unit 18
☐ chip away at	Unit 9	☐ open the door	Unit 14
☐ close in on	Unit 7	☐ opposed to	Unit 1
☐ come under fire	Unit 9	☐ pass around	Unit 18
☐ date back	Unit 6	☐ point of view	Unit 17
☐ decide on	Unit 6	☐ point out	Unit 3
☐ depending on	Unit 1	☐ pose a health risk	Unit 11
☐ die out	Unit 19	☐ put forward	Unit 16
☐ exposed to	Unit 3	☐ refer to	Unit 5
☐ first and foremost	Unit 3	☐ responsible for	Unit 10
☐ form the backbone of	Unit 20	☐ set someone apart	Unit 7
☐ from scratch	Unit 4	☐ show up	Unit 10
☐ get involved	Unit 10	☐ stand in for	Unit 5
☐ get to	Unit 15	☐ stand tall	Unit 13
☐ give up	Unit 4	☐ stick to	Unit 8
☐ go into	Unit 19	☐ stop off	Unit 8
☐ go out of one's way	Unit 14	☐ take over	Unit 5
☐ go through the roof	Unit 12	☐ take part in	Unit 20
☐ head on	Unit 13	☐ tap into	Unit 4
☐ hold true	Unit 12	☐ tend to	Unit 17
☐ in charge	Unit 14	☐ time on one's hands	Unit 8
☐ in the event of	Unit 1	☐ time-consuming	Unit 19
☐ in turn	Unit 11	☐ to one's heart's content	Unit 13
☐ just as	Unit 6	☐ up to date	Unit 2
☐ keep in check	Unit 18	☐ well-positioned	Unit 20

About the Author

Andrew E. Bennett holds an EdM (Master of Education) degree from Harvard University and a BA degree from UC Santa Cruz. He has studied seven languages. It's a life-long passion that began with a study of Spanish and continues with his ongoing studies of Chinese and Japanese.

Andrew has been involved in English education since 1993, both as a teacher and a writer. He has taught a variety of subjects, including English composition, business writing, English literature, and TOEFL preparation.

Andrew is the author of more than 30 English learning books, including classroom texts, supplementary books, self-study books, as well as TOEIC preparation texts. In addition to writing and teaching, he regularly attends ESL conferences and gives presentations to groups of teachers at schools and symposiums.

Central to Andrew's teaching philosophy is an emphasis on content. His work includes subjects from countries around the world, giving his writing an international flavor. Andrew also enjoys writing about cultural issues, as he is convinced of the vital link between language and culture.